Fiestas
for Four Seasons

Fiestas
for Four Seasons

Southwest Entertaining
with Jane Butel

JANE BUTEL

Photographs by Marcia Keegan

 Clear Light Publishers
Santa Fe, New Mexico

Library of Congress Cataloging-in-Publication Data

Butel, Jane.
    Fiestas for four seasons: Southwest entertaining with Jane Butel / Jane Butel.
        p.   cm.
    ISBN: 0-940666-72-3
    1. Cookery, American—Southwestern style.   2. Menus.   3. Entertaining.
    I. Title
    TX715.2.S69B877   1995
    641.5979—dc20   95-34069
                                                                                CIP

Typographical Design/Production: Vicki S. Elliott

❈ Contents

❧ Acknowledgments

Creating, testing and developing the menus and recipes for this cookbook has indeed been lots of fun—first, having the opportunity to work with my longtime associate, Marcia Keegan, has been wonderful! She has been the spirit behind getting this book into print. (Marcia and I first met in the early '60s when we were both in the food field here in Albuquerque, New Mexico. She was a Food Editor and I was in charge of Home Economics for the Electric Utility company.)

I also wish to acknowledge all the help and enthusiastic interest I have received from my husband Gordon, who was always willing to taste every new dish and give his ideas as well as my staff at my Southwestern Cooking School in Albuquerque.

The seasons are special in New Mexico and these recipes and menus were created to share this delightful difference!

I ❀ Southwestern Basics

Ingredients

Standard Preparations

Sauces and Salsas

Ingredients
The Four Seasons in Southwestern Cooking

An old European adage advises that if one always eats what is in season, then one's body will always be in tune with the climate. For example, the root vegetables of winter supposedly give the essential nutrition needed to brace the body for "the elements." The crisp lighter veggies of summer are just perfect for enjoying when one does not want to get bogged down with heavier, starchy foods.

Seasonal settings and decor for meals make for much more interesting dining. The ceremony of food is fun! With this spirit in mind, I sincerely hope you enjoy preparing all these menus!

The ingredients used in Mexican-southwestern cooking are simple and easily obtainable. In fact, there are probably fewer basic ingredients involved in preparing these dishes than in those of almost any other ethnic cuisine. Interestingly, this cuisine grew sophisticated in relative isolation and borrowed heavily from Mexican and New Mexican Indian sources, each of which used readily available ingredients, many of them indigenous to the area.

The most popular regional dishes have as their basis either chile or corn, which are both native products. Chiles are the major ingredients of the famous stew best known as just plain chili or chili con carne. Chiles are often used to flavor and thicken sauces and fillings, which, when combined with a corn or wheat tortilla, are the basis for numerous specialties such as *enchiladas, tacos, chimichangos, burritos,* and *flautas.*

The most popular southwestern flavorings are onion, garlic, tomato, Mexican oregano, cumin, and cilantro or coriander (the seeds of cilantro). Seeds and nuts are frequently used for flavor as well as thickening. Chocolate is also popular, though more often as an ingredient in drinks and main-dish sauces than in desserts.

Fruits and vegetables were relatively limited in early times. Corn was the staple, the essential grain used for tortillas and many vegetable dishes. Gourds and squash were used for vegetables dishes, soups, and stews. Beans were very popular, with the most common being the spotted pinto. More recently, many, many types of beans—including the spotted Anasazis, bolitos, and black beans are used. Fruits such as apples, apricots, and plums grew abundantly where there was water. Melons were always very popular together with some berries. Avocados have long been associated with Mexican and southwestern foods. Now, fresh and innovative fruits and vegetables are available in a very wide variety, particularly in farmers' markets.

Trends in Southwestern Cooking

The two most notable are low-fat and vegetarian. Low-fat is easily adjusted for in most southwestern foods or recipes. One word of caution is that "fat is flavor," and there is no adjusting for or getting around that fact.

In the low-fat preparation of meats, always select leaner cuts and use little or no fats in preparing them. Fats and oils can almost always be greatly reduced or eliminated, especially in sautéing or basting meats—instead, roast, broil or grill. Or if possible, smoke the meat in a smoker.

Eliminate fat-laden sauces. Almost none of the savory sauces in this book have any more than the minimal amount of fat needed to prepare them. An example is the red and green chile sauce recipes, both of which have the least possible fat for making the sauce work. An alternative would be to eliminate all fat and just reduce the sauce by simmering—a possibility.

The spiciness of the chiles edged with some sort of acid such as lime juice, vinegars, or wine will greatly reduce the desire for fat or large servings—both of which help with lowering fat and weight.

Cheeses and sour cream can be trimmed and substituted for or eliminated. For example, low-fat or no-fat sour cream and cheeses can be used. Yogurt can be substituted or blended with no-fat cottage cheese.

Side dishes can be made low-fat by just steaming them and using minimal or no fats for flavoring. Corn tortillas, freshly made or warmed are a very nutritious no-fat substitute for bread and butter. Eat them warm as they are with no butter!

For desserts, whipped cream, ice cream, and rich sauces can be omitted. Some of these are included in this book for flavor reasons, however. Fresh fruit, light custard and other low-fat desserts can be substituted if preferred.

Vegetarian cooking adapts itself easily to southwestern cooking. Beans, hearty vegetables, corn, and rice prepared various ways can substitute for the meat dishes and meat ingredients. Tofu can substitute for the cheeses, and sour cream, generally a garnish, can just be left out, depending on the type of vegetarianism being observed.

Beef, pork, and chicken are the standard meats—with game added, when available. Fish and shellfish, now found in many dishes, were once seldom encountered in the Southwest, although in Mexico they were abundant.

The breads of the region are quite simple but flavorful, and though time-consuming to make, they well reward the effort. The two most popular varieties are the range-top-baked corn or wheat *tortillas*, and the deep-fried *sopaipillas*, or Indian fry bread. Another favorite is a hearth bread that is generally formed into the shape of a bear claw. Sweet rolls, such as *moyettes* or *pan dulce*, are also uncomplicated and feature a basic butter and sugar topping, which sometimes includes cinnamon.

Desserts have always been simple and are often custard-based dishes, such as *natillas* or *flan*. These are sometimes complemented by fresh fruit or rich cookies or pastries. The more elaborate exceptions include *dulce* (sweet) *tamales* and sweet, nut-laden candies such as pralines.

Chiles

Chiles (the pods, as opposed to *chili*, the dish) provide the personality for the cuisine in the area both north and south of the Mexican border. Their wonderful qualities were first discovered by the Indians, who later shared their knowledge with the Spanish. Christopher Columbus, searching as he was for a new route to the East for the spice trade, thought he had found in the chile a valuable substitute for black peppercorns, and chiles have confusingly been called peppers ever since. They are in fact in the same vegetable family as potatoes, tomatoes, and eggplant. The Spanish eventually propagated the chile throughout the world, and today thousands of varieties of chiles have been recorded.

There are only four basic types of fresh chiles I use for New Mex/Tex-Mex cooking. Each is sold in both red and green forms; red chiles are sun-ripened green chiles. Green chiles are tarter and sometimes hotter than the red chiles, which contain natural sugar. Red chiles are usually sold dried, either as whole pods or in pure ground form. Pure ground chiles have a much broader range of uses than the more widely available chile powder. When buying ground chiles, always look for deep red color which signifies freshness. The brighter the color, for its type, the fresher. Do not buy standard commercial chile powder, which contains as much as 40 percent salt and 20 percent additives, which confuse the rich, natural flavor of the chiles. This compound was made to flavor beef for chili con carne and is limited in its flavor range.

The domestic New Mexican chile, which is medium hot, is the most commonly used, either fresh or dried. The hotter varieties of the north are quite different in both shape and color from the more abundant southern New Mexico chiles. The northern chiles are a brilliant, deep red and are generally sold as *caribe*, or *ristra* chiles (whole chiles on a string). They are considered the finest in New Mexico for red chile sauces, such as those used for making enchiladas.

The California or Anaheim chile is really a southern New Mexico chile and is about half as hot as the northern New Mexico types. This milder type, sold as pure ground chile, is terrific for creating a bright red, flavorful base, as it has the greatest thickening power. Hotter types of chiles can be added for piquancy in as punishing a quantity as you desire.

Outside the Southwest and Mexico, fresh jalapeño chiles have become generally available throughout the United States and Canada. Jalapeños grow in a broad range of climates and are very popular for adding piquancy to salsas. They are a stubby roundish chile that is hotter than the average New Mexican chile and thick fleshed. If not available fresh, they are almost always available pickled or *en escabeche* (page 25). Another favorite recipe for jalapeños is Homemade Jalapeño Jelly, (page 26).

Ripe jalapeños have long been smoked by the descendants of the Aztecs. Traditionally, they were smoked in banana leaves in deep earthen trenches. To this day, I prefer these dried jalapeños to the canned ones, which to me have a metallic taste. The best quality dried ones are brown and quite wrinkled and smell very smoky. These are not to be confused with the maroon-colored *mauras* or *mauritas*, which are mechanically dried and smoked, have little flavor, and produce a clear juice when stewed. Traditional jalapeños produce a mahogany-colored juice, which is quite flavorful. To reconstitute the dried chiles, they must be stewed in acidic water —water to barely cover to which 1 to 2 teaspoons acid such as vinegar, wine, or lime juice is added.

The fourth chile I use is one that gives real punch, the *pequin quebrado*. It is about the hottest of the chiles that still have the characteristic southwestern or Mexican chile flavor, and is generally sold crushed. It was this little guy, which measures only about the size of a little fingernail, that Columbus obtained from the Indians—and the rest is history.

MAIL ORDER SOURCE: Pecos Valley Spice Co., P.O. Box 964, Albuquerque, NM 87103; 1-800-473-TACO (8226) has all the pure chiles and corn masa products called for in my recipes.

Corn

For centuries corn has held its position on the highest gustatory pedestal. The ancient Indians worshiped the God of Corn and believed that man was created from corn dough, or masa. With this favored status, corn received much special care. Lacking modern refrigeration, the Aztecs learned that, once dried, corn could be stored almost indefinitely without spoiling, if generously sprinkled with lime. Their corn was not only cured with lime, it was also often stored in the web of limestone caves and caverns honeycombing the mountains of Mexico. The taste so ubiquitous in multitudes of Mexican corn dishes originated with this method of preservation.

Dried corn is traditionally white. Blue corn is popular in New Mexico, however, and has quite a different, richer flavor as a result of its curing. It is first smoked in adobe ovens fired with piñon and then lava-stone ground to a fine powder or flour, which is used in favorite dishes like blue cornbread, *rellenos* batter, *tamales*, and *tortillas*. Blue corn until recently was reserved basically for religious ceremonies and for feeding the fetishes or spirits. It provides complete nutrition: all the essential amino acids, vitamins, minerals, and other nutrients to maintain healthy bodily functions in humans. This claim can be made for few other foods, and not for any other corn. Yellow corn, the most popular color used in the United States, is more Texan than Mexican.

Posole, made from lime-treated whole kernels of mature white or blue corn, is the soul food and the mother process for corn served at all fiestas, rites, and Indian celebrations. All masa products are made from *posole*. Corn is served at most every southwestern meal. Fresh corn appears in summertime delights like green corn tamales, custards, and vegetable medleys.

Cheeses

In Tex-Mex cooking throughout the Southwest, Monterey Jack, or Jack blended equally with yellow, full-cream cheddar, is the most often used cheese. Monterey Jack cheese was developed in Monterey, California, where the best Jack is still produced. Top quality Jack is made of whole milk mozzarella blended with approximately 40 percent cheddar, and is formed into giant wheels that are generously coated with paraffin. Wisconsin Jack and most other commercial Jack cheeses are much firmer textured and less creamy and flavorful. They do grate better, but the tradeoff is generally not worth it if the Monterey is available.

Queso fresco is the traditional Mexican cheese. It is white, somewhat dry, and salty—a bit reminiscent of feta, which can be used as a substitute.

Most cheeses, unless low-fat or no-fat, are laden with fat. My recipes call for the optimum amount for flavor, but if you wish to cut fat and calories, reduce the amount of cheese to your preference.

Beans

The true southwestern bean is the pinto—a brown-speckled, grayish legume that cooks up to a firm, flavorful, almost nutlike taste. Cooked and mashed, pintos become *refritos*, "refried beans." Black beans have become popular in southwestern cooking, though were not traditionally used.

Shortening

Although lard is the traditional shortening of southwestern cooking, butter or bacon drippings are occasionally used. For cholesterol's sake (or any other) you may substitute margarine for solid shortening and vegetable oil for frying. The flavors and texture of the final dish, however, will not be the same.

For lower-cholesterol frying, select corn or soy oils or a blend of vegetable oils instead of frying in lard or butter, especially for deep frying. Canola is not a good choice, as it breaks down at the frying temperatures used in southwestern cooking (375° on average). Olive oil is good for some uses and will be called for in recipes where it is best. I personally prefer Spanish olive oil for its rich, fruity flavor. It is not used for deep frying as it has too low a smoking point.

Wherever possible within the various recipes, ways to reduce fat and frying will be pointed out.

Onions

The preferred onions for almost all cooking purposes are the large, round Spanish onions. White are best, with the yellow or purple (as long as they are sharp—not sweet) a second choice. An exception would be for use in a salad, where a milder flavor is sometimes preferable.

Garlic

Try to find the large, purplish cloves of Mexican garlic for the most pungent and full flavor. If you use other types of fresh garlic with smaller cloves, you should probably double the quantity called for in the recipes in this book. Figure that each clove should fill a generous ½ teaspoon or more.

Cilantro

Cilantro, a close relative of the parsley family (it can often be bought in greenmarkets as Chinese parsley), possesses a special clean, clear, pungent flavor that either makes close friends or adamant enemies. For those who appreciate its taste, the leaves of this aggressive herb are an invaluable addition to soups, salads, and relishes. Many like the seed (known as coriander in English) for flavoring sauces, salads, cakes, and baked goods. *(**Note:** In Mexico, culantro or cilantro is used to refer to both the seed and the green leaves. When shopping be certain to buy the correct form of the ingredient. In many Puerto Rican markets it is known as cilantrillo.)* A note when cooking with cilantro: always coarsely chop it and add at the last minute.

Honey

In the Southwest, honey has always been a very popular cooking ingredient, perhaps because some of the most aromatic of all blossom honeys are derived from the local cacti—specifically the *palo verde*, *saguaro*, and prickly pear. Each has a different potency—the *saguaro* being the mildest and the prickly pear the strongest. Other favorite blossom honeys in the area include the clovers, fruit trees, and mesquite. Try to select a good-quality aromatic honey for the recipes in this book, as its flavor will often dominate the completed dish.

Avocados

The very finest are the Haas, or old-fashioned Mexican alligator pears, which are pear-shaped and have a black, textured skin. They have the richest, most buttery texture and flavor and are the best base for guacamole and garnishes. The second best is the freckled, dark-green, pear-shaped *Fuertes*, which has a smaller neck than the Haas. The ones to avoid are the shiny green, smooth-skinned, round varieties, which are too sweet and watery.

When planning to use avocados, purchase them hard about 5 days ahead to allow them to ripen slowly. The best place for ripening is above your refrigerator, providing it is not in bright sunlight (which will "sunburn" an avocado, forming a dark brown spot where it is exposed). Another favorite method involves wrapping avocados in a brown paper bag and burying them in the flour bin. In fact, any dark, rather warm place is ideal. Avocados are ripe when their flesh yields to a firm press with your thumb; at this point, they can be kept in the refrigerator for several days.

The easiest way to peel an avocado is not to peel it! For making guacamole, just cut the fruit in half, remove the pit, and scoop out the flesh. For salads and garnishes, score the peel lengthwise with a very sharp knife in about six places; then, using the back of a spoon or the knife, take a section of the skin at a time and curl it back until it comes off.

Standard Preparations

Basic procedures are needed to prepare many of the popular southwestern ingredients. For example, green chiles must always be parched and peeled before using. Jalapeños and other small hot chiles are an exception—they can be eaten as is, minced very finely. Red chiles, if not bought ground, require special care to make the broth for use in sauces.

Tortillas prepared in various forms are basic to this cuisine and are best served freshly made.

Green Chile Parching

Green chiles freshly parched, or parched and frozen, are far superior to their canned equivalents. Canning always seems to impart a metallic taste and reduces the texture and flavor. Although freezing does soften the crisp texture, it does not impair the taste. Due to seasonality and perishability of chiles, freezing is often the only alternative. Green chiles are generally available from late June, when the first of the crop comes in, to late September, when they ripen and become red, signaling the end of the season.

Parching is necessary to remove the very leathery peel of fresh chiles. The process is easy, but be sure to wear rubber gloves or generously butter your hands to prevent a burn from the chile's irritating oils. Intense direct heat is needed to parch the peel, but take care to leave the flesh itself uncooked.

Immediate chilling of the parched chile halts the cooking process and causes the skin to blister away from the flesh. If freezing, freeze whole with the peel on for greatest flexibility of use. Parched green chiles freeze well for one year.

With a double oven range, you can parch a bushel of chiles in 1½ to 2 hours.

1. Wash the chiles, removing all sand and dirt. Leave the stem on, then pierce each once with a sharp knife, about 1 inch down from the stem.

2. For large quantities, cover the entire top rack of an electric oven with heavy foil; if using gas, cover the broiler rack. For smaller quantities, cover a cookie sheet.

3. Place the rack under an electric broiler 4 inches from the broiler unit; if using gas, place the rack on the top shelf.

4. After preheating the broiler, place a single layer of chiles on the foil. Allow each side to blister before rotating. Uniformly blister each chile for easy removal of the peel. As soon as each chile is parched, remove to the sink or a large bowl or tub of ice water. Immerse each, covering with a towel. Allow to cool, then either peel or package in airtight, vapor-proof plastic bags.

5. To peel, always start at the stem end and pull off strips of the peel. Blot dry between layers of paper towels before using. Keep the stem on for rellenos, but for other uses, remove it. For a milder taste, scrape out the seeds and veins with the dull side of a knife.

Notes: If parching only a few chiles, place each directly on a medium hot electric surface unit, or hold it with tongs or a meat fork over a gas burner.

A charcoal or gas grill works well also. If parching outdoors on a charcoal grill, place the rack about 4 inches above white-ashed coals. Watch the chiles carefully as they parch quickly.

In New Mexico, during the height of green chile season, enterprising chile growers and markets will offer to parch green chiles in blowtorch-fired rotating mesh drums. I do not agree with this practice; it produces inferior results at best and at worst can produce food poisoning resulting from the speed and method of handling.

Inferior results come from uneven handling of the parching and lack of chilling, which produce flesh that is yellow green, not bright green. The texture is not as desirable either—it is soft and mushy and thin fleshed, rather than crisp and thick fleshed.

Food poisoning can result from not washing the chiles, parching ones that are broken or half-rotten, then storing them in a warm plastic bag—germs incubate quickly while the chiles await bagging and freezing.

Basic Preparation of Red Chile Pods

If cooking with red chile pods, allow one to two pods per person. Rinse the pods with water, then remove the stems and shake out the seeds. Crush each chile and place in a shallow pan and roast in a 300° oven for about 10 to 15 minutes or until the color deepens and a roasted aroma develops. Do not roast too long or a burnt taste will develop. Place the roasted, crushed chiles in a saucepan with water to cover to about an inch above the tops of the chiles. Simmer for 30 minutes. Strain and use in the chile sauce recipes. (For speed, this mixture can be run through a blender instead of being strained.)

❈   ❈   ❈

"Bowl of Red"

This recipe has been in our family for three generations, ever since my Swedish maternal grandfather got it from an old Texas trail cook who worked herds of cattle from central Texas all the way to where the railroad ended in Dodge City, Kansas. It's great used as the chile in burritos, chimichangos, *and* casseroles and it is also the very best chili con carne to serve as is with "fixin's 'n mixin's" of coarsely grated mixed cheeses (Monterey Jack and cheddar), sour cream with fresh lime wedges, pequin que-brado, jalapeño nacho *slices, and chopped Spanish onions.*

Yield: 6 to 8 servings

2 tablespoons lard or melted beef fat
1 cup chopped Spanish onion (1 large)
3 pounds lean beef (chuck) cut in ½-inch squares
¼ cup mild ground chile
¼ cup hot ground chile
3 garlic cloves, minced
2 teaspoons or more freshly ground cumin
1 quart water
1½ teaspoons salt

1. Melt the lard or beef fat trimmings in a heavy pan. Add the onion.

2. Combine the beef with the chiles, garlic, and cumin. As soon as the onion becomes clear, not browned, remove pan from the surface unit so the chile does not burn; then add the beef mixture.

3. Stir in the water and bring to a boil, uncovered. Stew for an hour or so until the liquid begins to cook down and the meat is getting done. Taste the stock and add salt to taste, starting with 1½ teaspoons. Stew for about 3 hours or until bright red, thick, and flavorful. Taste and adjust seasonings. Add more ground cumin if desired, just before serving. .

Note: This recipe can be frozen for one year.

Corn Tortillas

Corn Tortillas were the earliest, made from lime-treated corn or masa harina. These were frequently made for every meal. They do freeze and are readily available in most American markets—but the best are still those freshly made at home.

Yield: 8 to 10 tortillas

2 cups corn masa harina, yellow, white, or blue
3/4 teaspoon salt
about 1 cup hot water

1. Using a medium-sized bowl, combine the masa and salt. Make a well in the center. Add the water all at once and stir.

2. Preheat a *comal* or *tapa* (a flat, seasoned griddle) to a medium high heat. If the *comal* or griddle is not pre-seasoned, rub on a bit of lard or oil with a paper towel and heat the pan to allow it to smoke.

3. Dough is the right consistency when a small ball will not crack when pressed between the palms. If it sticks to the palms, make it a bit drier by adding more masa. If it is too dry, cracks form on the sides of the ball; add a bit more hot water.

4. Press* each tortilla by taking a portion of dough the size of a small hen's egg and rolling it until round, then placing it on the bottom of the tortilla press on top of a piece of waxed paper cut the approximate size of the tortilla. Top with another piece of waxed paper.

5. Press down, watching carefully not to press too hard and make too thin a tortilla. The thickness should be thinner than 1/8 inch. Raise the lid of the press, lift off the tortilla, and remove the top piece of waxed paper. Repeat the process with each tortilla. Place each tortilla on the preheated seasoned *comal* (on the surface unit or burner) and bake until the top feels warm and is slightly bubbled up. Turn and lightly brown the second side—it takes only a few seconds. Keep warm until serving.

*The easiest way to make successful corn tortillas is to use a tortilla press, available at Mexican specialty stores or by mail order from Pecos Valley Spice Co., PO Box 964, Albuquerque, NM 87103; 1-800-473-TACO (8226).

Soft Wheat Tortillas

Wheat tortillas, introduced by the Spanish and popularized in northern Mexico, are today the staple bread of the New Mexicans and other regional descendants of the Spanish. Even more than corn tortillas, they are at their very best when homemade: store-bought are never as fresh or flavorful. Once you acquire the knack of kneading, rolling, and baking them—pointers are included in the following recipe—you'll find you prefer to make your own whenever possible. If you don't have the time to bake tortillas fresh, look for commercial tortillas that are creamy colored, very fresh looking, and not dry and crinkled around the edges. Also, look for tortillas with small brown baking spots—larger spots indicate too-rapid baking. Warm them in packets of foil, placing no more than 6 tortillas in each package. Heat at 350° for 10 to 15 minutes, but no longer, or they will dry out.

Yield: 8 to 12 six- to eight-inch tortillas

4 cups unbleached flour
1½ teaspoons salt
2 teaspoons baking powder
Pinch of sugar
¼ cup lard or butter
1½ cups warm water

1. Carefully measure the flour, spooning it into the dry measuring cup and leveling it off. Do not scoop the flour. Place all the dry ingredients in a large mixing bowl and stir until well blended. Then cut in the lard, using a pastry blender, mixer, or your hands.

2. Make a well in the center, add about half the water, and mix well. Continue adding water, a little at a time, until a smooth, cohesive dough is formed.

3. Knead the dough until it is very smooth and quite firm and springy and will no longer cling to your hands. If too moist or too dry it will never knead to this stage. Adjust, if necessary, by adding more water or flour.

4. Cover and let stand in a warm place to rest until a large hole is left in the dough when punched—15 to 30 minutes. Meanwhile, shortly after the dough has started to rest, heat a seasoned cast-iron *comal* or *tapia* (a flat seasoned griddle) or other griddle, or a frying pan, or a stove lid, to medium heat on a burner. Lacking any of these, heat a stainless steel or other heavy griddle that will hold lots of heat and speed the baking.

5. Divide the dough into balls the size of an egg. Then stretch each into a circle, one at a time, holding it up and pulling out the dough. Twist the edges into small curls over one finger at a time, to create an edge that the Spanish-descendant new Mexicans call *repulgar,* which is the same edging used for empanadas and pie pastries.

6. Roll each tortilla with a small rolling pin called a *bollillo*, the Spanish name for a rolling pin that is 2 inches in diameter and about 8 inches long. This ensures the best control over the very firm, springy dough. Use the least possible flour on the board for the best texture and flavor. Roll each into a thin, round disk about ¼ inch thick and about 8 inches in diameter or as big as desired.

7. To bake, place the tortillas one at a time on the heated *comal* or griddle. Each side is done when it bubbles up and there are dark brown flecks; then turn to cook the second side. The baked tortilla should have no shiny spots, as they indicate underbaking. When done, place them on a plate covered with a linen towel and keep them stacked, one on another. Serve warm.

Variations: Use ½ or 2 cups whole wheat flour and 2 cups white flour for whole wheat tortillas. For less fat, lard or butter can be reduced to 3 tablespoons, even to 2 tablespoons. Use the least possible flour on the board for best texture and flavor. Roll, pressing out from the center and turning so as to create a smooth, evenly round tortilla—it will require lots of downward pressure to roll out. A wooden or marble pastry board no higher than 32 inches is best for rolling them on, as long as it is not too far from where they are to be baked.

❧   ❧   ❧

Baking Tostadas and Fresh Tortilla Tacos

To save approximately 25 calories per whole fried tortilla, bake them. They will be tougher and not as flavorful, however. To do this, preheat the oven to 400°, then cut the tortillas (corn in fourths or wheat in sixths or eighths). Sprinkle or spray the surface of the tortillas with water or oil. Place them on a baking sheet and place in the oven. Bake until crisp. Serve warm.

❧   ❧   ❧

Fresh Tortilla Tacos

For fresh tortilla tacos, serve warm, freshly made (as above), preferably homemade corn tortillas. Guests can layer the chilied meat, onion, lettuce, cheese, tomato and salsa. This is the traditional Mexican taco.

Tostado Frying

To fry the "edible baskets," the simplest way is to use a purchased tostado-frying basket, which comes in two parts. Following the manufacturer's instructions, place a tortilla between the two parts of the fryer and fry in preheated 375° oil in an electric deep fryer or use a thermometer in a deep pot of oil and carefully watch the temperature.

Or create your own, by piercing an empty metal can that allows at least a one-inch margin at the edges of the tortilla. (Be sure to remove the label from the can.) With a beverage opener, pierce four holes evenly spaced around the bottom; on the side of the can close to the bottom, pierce four alternating holes spaced halfway between the bottom holes. Using 375° hot oil as described above, place a corn or flour tortilla in the hot oil. Hold the can you created in the center of the tortilla, firmly push the bottom down on the tortilla, but take care not to push to the bottom of the fryer. As soon as the rapid bubbling subsides, remove the tostado from the hot oil and invert it on a paper towel covered cooling rack. Place a wad of paper towel in the hollow of the upside down tostado.

❦   ❦   ❦

Frying Tostadas

Here is a recipe for frying tostadas—quartered, crisply fried corn chips. (Tostadas have the feminine "a" ending to indicate that they are made from a portion of the tortilla, *while the "o" ending of* tostado *indicates that a whole tortilla was used.) The rewards of preparing tostadas yourself are great! Almost all packaged varieties are filled with extra calories, since most commercial manufacturers shortcut the frying process and leave in enormous amounts of retained fat.*

Yield: 4 dozen

2 quarts corn or vegetable oil
1 dozen corn tortillas (any color)
Salt

1. Use an electric deep-fat fryer, if available; if not, use a large 5- to 8-quart cooking pot over medium-high heat, with a candy thermometer to measure the temperature of the oil. Heat the oil to 375°. The fat must be maintained at 375° for crisp, dry, non-fatty tostadas.

2. With a very sharp knife, make 4 cuts at right angles to each other through the stack of tortillas, cutting almost but not completely through the center. This method saves the trouble of frying four separate pieces and fishing out each individual tostada. It also guarantees more uniform frying.

3. Fry a few tortillas at a time, taking care to let the oil return to 375°. Fry until the bubbling stops and each tortilla has become crisp.

4. Drain on several layers of absorbent toweling set on a cooling rack. While still somewhat warm, tap each tortilla in the center and the four pieces will separate. Place the pieces in a paper bag, sprinkle with some salt, and shake. Serve warm for best flavor with freshly prepared salsas.

Crisp Corn Taco Shells

Crisp taco shells are purely American! They appeal to the kid in all of us and are quite popular. The best are home fried just before serving. When you fry your own, you can fry as many as three kinds of corn—yellow, white, and blue. You can make them in the familiar U shape described in this recipe, in the basket shape (see Tostado Frying on page 22), or in a flat tostado shape.

Although you can fry taco shells the day before and rewarm them, try to fry them fresh about 2 hours before serving. Use the two-tong technique, or, easier still, buy taco frying tongs, which are showing up in more and more gourmet and department stores. You can buy taco shells ready-made— but you will be much more limited in the flavors and varieties available.

Yield: 12 shells

1 dozen corn tortillas
2 quarts vegetable oil

1. Place several layers of paper towels under an upright wire taco rack. If a rack is unavailable, make enough small wads of paper toweling, about 1½ inches in diameter, to fill each traditional U shaped taco.

2. Meanwhile, heat the oil to 375° in a deep-fat fryer, or in a 5-quart heavy pot, using a candy thermometer to aid in maintaining the temperature, which is critical for good results.

3. To fry the traditional U shapes, place a tortilla in the taco fryer, making sure that the side of the tortilla with the least browned edges is on the outside.

4. Then immerse in the hot oil until the bubbles subside, usually about 15 seconds. Fry each until it is crisp, dry, and not shiny looking, which indicates undercooking. Do not overcook, as the flavor and color will not be as good.

5. As soon as each is fried, remove with tongs and drain—either on the rack or on its side with a wad of toweling inside, which is important to drain the fat as well as to keep the taco shell from folding together.

6. If frying them with two tongs, grasp the two opposite sides of the tortilla, making certain that the side with the least browned appearance is on the outside—a tip to make bending easier and reduce the risk of breaking. Submerge the tortilla in hot oil holding the tortilla in a "U-shape," and fry until the bubbles subside and it is crisp, not browned. Drain as above.

7. To create flat tacos or tostados, just hold one side of the tortilla with your tongs and fry until crisp. Drain as above, omitting the wads of paper, but topping each with additional paper toweling.

Carne Deshebrada
(Shredded Beef or Pork)

The traditional Mexican filling for tacos, enchiladas, flautas, and the like is shredded meat, rather than a chilied sauce laced with meat, as is standard for Tex-Mex dishes.

Yield: 12 servings

*3 pounds beef chuck, pork shoulder or butt,
    or stewed chicken*
1½ teaspoons salt
6 peppercorns
2 bay leaves
1 medium Spanish onion, quartered
2 garlic cloves, coarsely chopped
4 cups water

1. Using a Dutch oven or large heavy cooking pot, brown the beef or pork until the outside edges are dark brown.

2. Add the remaining ingredients and simmer, covered, for 2 hours, or until fork tender. Let remain covered in juices until cool. Then, using two forks or your fingers, shred the meat, discarding the bones and any excess fat.

Note: For chicken, stew whole chicken in 2 quarts chicken stock to which 2 teaspoons jalapeño pickle juice or vinegar have been added. Stew covered for 45 minutes or until the joints wiggle. Allow to cool in the stock, then remove the flesh from the bones and skin.

Deshebrada Fry Mixture

*2 tablespoons butter, lard, or bacon drippings
    (more if meat is dry)*
4 garlic cloves, minced
2 medium Spanish onions, finely chopped
2 to 3 jalapeño chiles, minced (optional)

Melt the fat in a large heavy skillet. Add the garlic and onion. As soon as they start to become golden, add the shredded meat and stir fry until it becomes browned on the edges, about 15 minutes. Add jalapeños toward the end of cooking. If the meat becomes too dry, add some of the meat broth to moisten.

Jalapeños en Escabeche

This recipe for pickled jalapeños, from a dear friend in Albuquerque, is one of the best I know. It is especially suited to small batch preparation, but you can certainly "batch it up" if you wish. The only tedious part is the preparation of the chiles, but the light sautéing in sesame oil adds excellent flavor, and serves to tame them a bit. You can use these as a relish, or as an ingredient in sauces, salsas, and guacamole.

Yield: 3 to 4 pints

3 medium-sized carrots, peeled and sliced
*   ¼ inch thick*
1 cup cider vinegar, 5 percent acidity
1 cup water
2 medium Spanish white onions, very thinly sliced
*   and separated into rings*
6 garlic cloves
1 teaspoon salt
2 teaspoons Mexican oregano
3 large, whole bay leaves, preferably fresh
2 pounds small to medium-sized firm-fleshed,
*   blemish-free jalapeño chiles, halved, seeded,*
*   washed, and blotted dry*
½ cup sesame oil

1. Cook the carrots in a small amount of salted water until slightly tender. Drain and cool and set aside.

2. Combine the vinegar, water, onions, garlic, and salt in a non-reactive saucepan. Cook until onions are slightly tender. Add oregano and bay leaves. Bring just to a boil.

3. Sauté the jalapeños in the sesame oil until the skins blister. Peel the jalapeños and add the carrots to the vinegar mixture. Cool and refrigerate for 24 hours before serving.

Note: When preparing the chiles, always be very careful either to wear rubber gloves or very generously butter your fingertips and palms to prevent a chile burn, which lasts up to 24 hours. A melon ball scoop or a grapefruit knife helps to scrape out the seeds and veins easily.

Homemade Jalapeño Jelly

There are many jalapeño jellies on the market, but few are as good as the one this recipe yields—a lovely, richly flavored jelly that captures the freshness of chiles.

Yield: Five 6-ounce jars

3 cups ripe red bell peppers
5 fresh jalapeño chiles, finely chopped
1½ cups cider vinegar
6½ cups sugar
6 ounces bottled liquid pectin

1. Boil 5 clean jelly jars in at least 1 inch of water while making the jelly.

2. Chop the peppers and chiles by hand or use a food processor or blender to process into a medium grind. Combine with the vinegar and sugar in a large, heavy saucepan and boil for 30 minutes.

3. Allow to cool for 10 minutes. Stir in the pectin and boil for 2 minutes or until jelled. To test, dip a metal spoon in at right angles to the surface of the jelly and lift it about a foot above the surface. While still at right angles, allow the drops to "sheet" off. If they do not come together and sheet off, continue boiling and test again.

4. Remove the jelly from the heat, skim, and allow it to cool. Stir so that the peppers and chiles are evenly distributed; carefully ladle into sterilized jars. Clean the inside of each jar around the top with a hot cloth dipped in boiling water. When cool, seal with paraffin.

Guacamole

I've often been credited with making "perfect guacamole" using this recipe!

Yield: 6 servings

3 ripe Haas avocados
1 Mexican lime, halved, plus juice to taste
⅓ cup finely chopped Spanish onion
¼ cup cubed red ripe tomato
3 garlic cloves, minced
¾ teaspoon salt
1 medium fresh jalapeño, or to taste, minced
¼ cup coarsely chopped cilanto, optional

1. Halve each avocado and scoop the flesh into a shallow mixing bowl. Cut into ½ inch squares, using two knives.

2. Combine with 1½ teaspoons (or to taste) lime juice, the onion, tomato, garlic, salt, and jalapeño, being careful not to crush the avocado. Taste and adjust the seasonings. Fold in the cilantro.

Sauces and Salsas

Mastering the sauces for this cuisine takes you a long way toward flavorful southwestern or Mexican food. The cooked sauces are easily and quickly made. Chile-laden sauces must always be slowly simmered. The following recipes are each my favorite for the type. The Red Chile Sauce prepared this way with pure ground New Mexican chiles is so good; always consistent and it can be made right on top of sautéed ground beef, incorporating the beef into the sauce. Note the variation. I much prefer using the pure ground chiles, as they are much more convenient, flavorful, and consistent than whole pods.

Salsas in southwestern/Mexican dishes are freshly made, generally using fresh, uncooked ingredients. There are exceptions, such as cooking tomatillos to give them a better consistency. And using canned tomatoes means the salsa will keep for a longer period of time.

Salsas dollar for dollar now outsell catsup as Americans' favorite condiment. And no wonder! They are so flavorful, healthful, and easy to make. You can vary salsas greatly, substituting favorite fruits and vegetables for the tomatoes and substituting different chiles for the ones called for.

Red Chile Sauce

This sauce—sometimes called enchilada *sauce—is probably the most frequently served sauce in the Southwest. Although it is sold canned, which is always dreadful, and frozen, which is barely acceptable, you can easily whip up a homemade version in 5 minutes, with another 15 to 30 minutes of simmering. The critical ingredient is pure, ground red New Mexico chile. The best color and texture come from blending mild chiles with hotter ones. Mild chiles have a higher starch level, which acts as a thickener, and are a deeper almost bluish red color, which blends beautifully with the orange-red hotter chiles, which supply the heat.*

You can easily adjust the piquancy to taste—even at the dining table—by making a mild sauce and providing a bowl of the ground, pure, hot New Mexico chile. Don't ever make this sauce with commercial chile powder, as it will be briny, dark, and stale-tasting due to the salt and chemicals that have been added.

You'll find this sauce terrific over enchiladas, burritos, chimichangos, *eggs, hamburgers, pork chops,* and *rellenos. For convenience, freeze in 1- to 2-cup portions, which will keep well for up to 8 months.*

Yield: 3 cups

¼ cup butter, lard, or solid shortening
¼ cup flour
¼ cup pure mild southern New Mexico chile powder
½ cup pure hot New Mexico chile powder
¼ teaspoon ground cumin
Pinch Mexican oregano
2½ cups well-flavored beef stock, or water
3 teaspoons salt, or to taste (if not using stock)
1 garlic clove, minced

1. Melt the butter, lard, or shortening in a heavy saucepan over low heat; then stir in the flour. When it is lightly browned, remove from the heat. When the pan has cooled slightly, thoroughly stir in the chile powder.

2. Add the cumin and oregano, then stir in about 1 cup of the beef stock. When well blended, return to the heat and stir, adding the remaining stock, a little at a time. Season to taste with the salt (if using) and garlic and simmer for at least 10 minutes—up to 30 minutes over low heat—until the sauce thickens and the flavors blend. Use as desired or freeze.

Variation: For beef enchiladas, brown 1 pound of hamburger first, omitting the lard. Then add the flour and proceed with the recipe.

Hot Green Chile Sauce

Hot green chile sauce is popular both in New Mexico and California, where so many green chiles are grown. At its best when made with freshly parched green chiles, it is a great sauce with pork, chicken, or seafood, and with traditional dishes like enchiladas, chimichangos, burritos, *or eggs. Canned green chiles can be substituted, but the flavor will be less pronounced.*

Yield: 3 cups

2 tablespoons lard, butter, or solid shortening
1/2 cup finely chopped Spanish onion
1/4 cup flour
2 cups rich chicken broth
1 cup chopped or sliced green chiles that have been parched, peeled, and deseeded (see page 17)
2 garlic cloves, minced
Pinch of ground cumin
3/4 teaspoon salt, optional

1. Melt the fat in a heavy saucepan. Stir in the onion and cook until it becomes clear. Stir in the flour.

2. When the mixture turns lightly golden, gradually add the broth, cooking and stirring until the sauce thickens slightly. Add the remaining ingredients except salt and simmer over low heat for about 30 minutes, until the flavors blend and the sauce is thickened. Taste and adjust flavor.

Chile con Queso

Fast food operations have popularized hot nacho cheese sauce, which is not nearly as flavorful or colorful as this dish, on which it is based. Traditionally, chile con queso has been served warm as a dunk for tostadas, but it's also very good over hamburgers, eggs, chimichangos, and other southwestern specialty dishes—including fajitas.

Yield: 1 quart

⅓ cup soy-based vegetable oil

1 cup finely chopped onion

2 cloves garlic, minced

2 tablespoons flour

1½ cups evaporated milk (evaporated skim is fine)

2 fresh medium-sized tomatoes, chopped (about ½ cup)

2 pounds processed American cheese, cubed

½ cup grated full cream yellow cheddar

½ cup grated Monterey Jack cheese

2 to 4 fresh, finely minced jalapeño chiles, stems and seeds removed (use smaller amount first)

1. Heat the oil over medium low heat in a heavy saucepan. Add the onion and garlic and cook until the onion becomes clear. Stir in the flour, mixing well.

2. Gradually add the evaporated milk, stirring, and cook until the mixture thickens. Add the remaining ingredients and cook over very low heat until the cheeses have all melted and the mixture is thick and smooth. Add jalapeños to suit taste.

3. Serve with warm tostadas or as a sauce. The sauce can be frozen for up to 4 months. For this, you may wish to package in 1-cup containers.

Note: Reduced fat cheeses and evaporated skim make this a much lower fat recipe.

Fresh Garden Salsa

Fresh as a garden bouquet! When you have a bit of extra time, the sophistication of the flavors and the versatility of this salsa are well worth the effort. This is one of my very favorites, which I first developed for a chain of restaurants and then set about perfecting for my own pleasure. Please hand chop the ingredients—it's worth the effort. Machine chopping will yield a less attractive salsa and it will have a bitter flavor.

Yield: 28 ounces (enough for 24 tacos or servings)

2 cups canned whole, good-quality tomatoes,
    drained and coarsely chopped
1/3 cup finely diced, fresh, red ripe tomato, unpeeled
2 tablespoons red wine vinegar
1 tablespoon finely diced Spanish onion
2 tablespoons freshly squeezed lime juice
2 teaspoons minced flat-leaf parsley
1 1/4 teaspoons sea or kosher salt
1 garlic clove, minced
1/4 cup water
1 tablespoon pickled jalapeño juice
2 tablespoons minced fresh chives
1 small jalapeño chile, minced (either fresh or canned)
2 New Mexican green chiles, parched, peeled, and
    diced (see page 17), or use 2 canned
    green chiles, diced
1/3 cup diced green bell pepper
1/4 teaspoon granulated sugar
1/4 teaspoon Mexican oregano
1/4 teaspoon cumin

1. Put all the ingredients in a glazed pottery or glass bowl and gently toss and stir to blend evenly.

2. Cover and refrigerate overnight, if possible, or at least 4 hours.

3. Serve as a table sauce, taco sauce, or over any grilled meat. If any is left over after three days, it can be added to 2 tablespoons melted sweet butter in a medium hot sauté pan and cooked and stirred to create a ranchero sauce for serving over eggs to make Huevos Rancheros. Or it can be frozen for later use for up to 3 months. Or use to flavor a vinaigrette salad dressing.

Cold Salsa Verde

Here is a very traditional green sauce that is excellent over chicken, seafood, or pork dishes, and is also frequently served as a table relish. Tomatillos (Mexican green tomato-like fruit) are called for here to give the sauce its traditional flavor; they are increasingly available at gourmet and chain food stores and Mexican specialty shops.

Yield: 1 pint

*2 cups raw, quartered **tomatillos** or 1 can (10 ounces) undrained tomatillos*
½ cup coarsely chopped Spanish onion
2 tablespoons fresh cilantro leaves
1 fresh jalapeño chile, or to taste
½ teaspoon salt

Steam the *tomatillos* in boiling water until tender, about 8 minutes, or open a can and drain. Place all ingredients in a blender or food processor. Puree them, then adjust seasonings and piquancy. This sauce is predictably hot.

❦ ❦ ❦

Creamy Salsa Verde

Amy, my daughter, has probably been my greatest and most enduring fan of this salsa. Its spicy, rich flavor, cooled by a creamy base, makes it perfect as a topper for tacos or as a dip for vegetables and snacks.

Yield: 1¼ cups

½ cup sour cream
½ cup mayonnaise
⅓ cup Cold Salsa Verde (recipe above; or substitute any other favorite green salsa)
1 tablespoon freshly squeezed lime juice
Sprinkle of caribe (or other crushed dried red chile), optional

Combine all ingredients except the caribe and allow to blend together in the refrigerator for at least 1 hour. Sprinkle with caribe before serving.

Santa Fe Salsa

This is the salsa that made a New Mexican restaurant in Santa Fe famous, but beware: It is the hottest of all. The sharp, tangy flavor is often a favorite of those who like their salsas hot, like myself. Serve with warm tostadas to take you back to the capital city of New Mexico, the "Land of Enchantment."

Yield: 1 pint

2 cups canned whole tomatoes, undrained and
*   coarsely crushed with a fork*
1 tablespoon or more crushed pequin quebrado chile*
4 teaspoons freshly squeezed lime juice
4 teaspoons cider vinegar
4 garlic cloves, minced
1/2 teaspoon Mexican oregano
1/2 teaspoon cumin
1 teaspoon crushed cilantro seeds (coriander)
1 teaspoon salt

1. Combine all the ingredients in a pottery or glass bowl, adding the pequin 1 teaspoon at a time to make certain that you will not get the salsa too hot.

2. Taste and adjust seasonings. Let stand 30 minutes at room temperature and serve. Can be stored for several days in the refrigerator. Do not freeze.

   *If *pequin* is unavailable, use a crushed red chile, preferably very hot.

❊   ❊   ❊

Salsa Fresca

The basis of all fresh table sauces, salsa fresca, literally translated, means "fresh sauce." Although there are many, many more sophisticated versions of this salsa, I still like it best at its simplest, as either a dipping sauce for warm tostadas or over hamburgers on tarragon-basil buttered buns. Do make it an hour or less before serving, as it is at its best very fresh. This is the original salsa!

Yield: 3 cups

1 cup finely diced red, ripe tomato, excess juice
*   and seeds removed*
1 cup finely diced Spanish onion, preferably red
*   and white mixed*
1 cup finely diced green chiles, preferably New
*   Mexico type, that have been parched, peeled,*
*   and deseeded (see page 17)*
2 garlic cloves, finely minced
1 teaspoon salt
1/2 cup coarsely chopped cilantro

Combine all the ingredients in an earthenware or porcelain bowl. Stir gently and set aside for at least 30 minutes before serving.

II ❋ Spring

Spring Blossoms Brunch

✤

M E N U

Mango Mimosas

*Blue Corn-Toasted Piñon Nut Waffles
with Tropical Fruit*

Glazed Smoked Pork Chops

*Fresh Strawberry Meringues
with Candied Violets*

Latté

✤

When the blossoms start bursting forth over the fruit trees and in the flower beds, what a perfect time to have a lazy weekend morning brunch. Spring is the season of nostalgia. Try to stage this brunch where the blossoms are in clear view—such as on a porch or patio. Lacking either or if in a major metropolitan area, still bring the season inside with a bountiful centerpiece of spring blossoms, such as lilacs accentuated with Oriental poppies, iris, or apple blossoms—whatever you can lay your hands on.

Don't be skimpy with the blossoms. Create bouquets everywhere, a moderate-sized low one for the dining table and one in the living room near the entry. Put them in the kitchen and even in the bathrooms. If possible, tuck a blossom in your hair or on a lapel.

An old fashioned feeling is comfy and easily set up with a lace or linen table cloth. What about that heirloom your grandmother or favorite aunt gave you? If using an heirloom, you may wish to use pastel place mats on top or pastel runners, fashioned from scarves or yard goods.

Clear glass plates or any coordinating plates with a pastel, springlike look are best. For the mimosas, use your tallest champagne glasses, such as flutes.

Day Before (or earlier):

Prepare the meringues.

Set the table.

Set out the waffle baker and skillet
for the pork chops.

Two hours before:

Peel, slice, and divide the mango for the
mimosas and the waffles.

Prepare the waffle batter.

Set the fruited yogurt and honey for serving
with the waffles on the table.

Hull, slice and sweeten the strawberries. Place
the pork chops in the skillet. Start pan grilling
30 minutes before the guests arrive.

Set meringues on serving plates.

At serving time:

Serve the mimosas.

Heat the waffle baker.

Warm the plates in a 200° oven.

Turn heat off under the chops when they
are browned in places and still juicy.

Prepare the coffee and heat milk for the lattés.

Mango Mimosas

*Mimosas always make for a festive brunch. Here instead
of the predictable orange juice, we've used mango.*

Yield: 6 servings

1/2 medium mango, peeled and sliced crosswise
1 fifth champagne

Using champagne glasses, pour about an inch of champagne in each glass. Then divide the mango pieces
among the glasses, placing about 3 to 4 in each. Fill
each glass with champagne to within about an inch of the
top and serve.

Blue Corn-Toasted Piñon Nut Waffles with Tropical Fruits

These have a full flavor and are very springlike. Use whatever berries or fruits are plentiful and good quality.

Yield: 6, 9-inch waffles

2 eggs
2 cups buttermilk
1/3 cup vegetable oil
1 cup blue corn flour
1 cup all-purpose flour
1 teaspoon baking soda
1 1/2 teaspoon baking powder
3/4 teaspoon salt
3 tablespoons toasted piñon nuts, coarsely chopped
1/2 cup fresh blueberries
1/2 mango, sliced and coarsely chopped
   (the other half used in mimosas)
1 small banana, thinly sliced

1. If serving immediately, heat the waffle iron; otherwise heat just before serving. Beat eggs, using a mixer or food processor. Add the buttermilk and oil and beat until well combined.

2. Add the flour, baking soda, baking powder, salt, and nuts and mix well. Using about 1/3 cup of batter at a time, pour on preheated waffle iron. Sprinkle with 1/6 of the three fruits. Cover and bake until done. Serve with butter and syrup or honey and fruited yogurt.

Glazed Smoked Pork Chops

Smoked Pork Chops were first introduced to me in Bavaria Germany, and they were so heavenly, I've been preparing them ever since. If you do not want a glaze, just place them in a heavy cold skillet and heat to a medium heat and cook until the first side is browned a bit, turn and cook the second side. The glaze is fun though.

Yield: 6 servings

6 smoked pork chops
3 tablespoons orange marmalade

1. Place the pork chops in a heavy cold skillet, then spread each with about 3/4 teaspoon marmalade. Place on medium heat and cook for about 12 to 15 minutes.

2. Check one chop to determine whether any browning has occurred. When browned, turn and spread the second side with marmalade. Add a bit of water to the pan as the second side begins to cook to deglaze the pan a bit and allow the marmalade to glaze each chop. Cook the second side about 10 minutes or until lightly browned and glazed.

Fresh Strawberry Meringues with Candied Violets

*What could be more like spring than juicy, red ripe, freshly picked strawberries? Topped
with meringue rounds, they are pretty, delicious, and light.*

Yield: 6 servings

TOPPING

2 pints fresh strawberries
1/2 cup granulated sugar or to taste
2 tablespoons Grand Marnier
18 candied violets or fresh violets

MERINGUES

6 egg whites
1/4 teaspoon salt
1 teaspoon white vinegar
1 teaspoon Mexican vanilla
2 cups granulated sugar

1. Lightly wash the strawberries without soaking them. Cut them into slices and sprinkle with the sugar and the Grand Marnier. Stir to blend; taste and adjust for sweetness.

2. To make the meringues, using an electric mixer, beat the whites until soft peaks form. Add the salt, vinegar, vanilla, and 1/2 cup sugar and beat until the meringue is soft. Add the rest of the sugar slowly as the mixer beats. Scrape the sides and under the beaters and beat on high speed until the meringue forms very stiff peaks.

3. Preheat the oven to 275°. Place brown paper on cookie sheets. Using a pastry tube or a tube cut from waxed paper, form 6 meringue circles, each about 4 to 5 inches across, and about 1½ inches high. Also make 6 small meringue "buttons," about an inch across. Bake for an hour and a half or until they are very firm. Turn off the oven and leave the meringues in the oven with the door closed for another hour. Remove and cool on racks.

4. To serve, using crystal plates, place 1/6 of the strawberries in a puddle on each plate. Center with a meringue circle and a "button" on the very center. Scatter the violets on the center.

Latté

*Latté is very popular in the Northwest and the craze spread across the country. It really
is no different from the café au lait that many of us were served as children.*

Yield: 6 servings

6 cups freshly brewed coffee
6 cups hot milk
1/4 cup sugar, optional
Freshly ground cinnamon

Heat the milk in a heavy saucepan with a pouring spout, if possible. Stir in the sugar. To serve, pour the coffee and the milk simultaneously into 6 large mugs. Top with a sprinkle of cinnamon.

A Spicy Lunch for a Rainy Day

M E N U

Strawberry Spritzers

Black Bean Salsa with Tortilla Toasts

*Herb-Basted Grilled Rib Lamb Chops
with Mint Tomatillo Salsa
on Seared Red Chard*

*Roasted Garlicky Mashed Potatoes
with Wild Mushrooms*

Deep Dish Peach Pie

Espresso

Spring rains are inevitable and definitely do bring the spring flowers. But during a rainy spell, right when our hearts are beginning to sing and we yen for those balmy spring days, everyone needs a cheery "pick-me-up"—a perfect opportunity to schedule a luncheon such as this one.

If the day is particularly gloomy, why not plan to serve lunch in front of a crackling fire to celebrate the end of winter? If the sun shines, enjoy it. If it's warm enough, set the table on the porch or even the patio.

Celebrate spring with spring flowers, such as violets strewn over the top of the table (at the last minute) along with a low centerpiece of jonquils, forsythia, tulips, and other spring flowers. Select your favorite yellow and white table linens or ones that will complement the spring flowers. A yellow and white quilt, sheet or even runners of yard goods would look great. Your plates should be simple— white or yellow and white.

This menu is less time consuming than many, especially if you stage the preparation—making the Black Bean Salsa with Tortilla Toasts ahead along with the pie.

Day before (or more):

Prepare the Black Bean Salsa.
Bake the Tortilla Toasts.
Prepare and bake the Deep Dish Peach Pie.
Rinse the chard and place in cloth or a bag.
Soak the wild mushrooms if using dried.
While baking the pie, roast the garlic.
Prepare the Mint Tomatillo Salsa.

Two hours before:

Arrange the centerpiece.
Prepare the herb baste and baste the lamb chops.
Start the fire in the grill one hour ahead.
Prepare the mashed potatoes.
Arrange the Black Bean Salsa with the
   Tortilla Toasts.

Chill the wine glasses for the spritzers and rinse
   and prepare the strawberries.
One half hour before serving, warm the dinner
   plates in 200° oven.
Set up the coffee preparation.

At serving time:

Serve the spritzers with the Black Bean Salsa and
   Tortilla Toasts.
Grill the lamb chops, meanwhile searing the
   chard.
Serve the lamb on the chard with the salsa and
   potatoes.
Warm the pie in the oven where you warmed
   the dinner plates.
Prepare the coffee to serve with the pie.

Strawberry Spritzers

Spritzers are light and quite refreshing as a luncheon eye opener!

Yield: 6 drinks

2 fresh limes
1 fifth Reisling or other wine compatible with fruit
1 33.8 fluid ounce bottle of seltzer
6 large fresh strawberries

Selecting your favorite tall white wine glasses, squeeze a sixth of a lime in each. Equally divide the wine among the glasses, topping off with enough seltzer to come to within an inch of the top. Garnish each with a strawberry, partially sliced and perched on the side of each glass.

Black Bean Salsa with Tortilla Toasts

Black beans lend themselves to spicy flavors and are quite wonderful in this somewhat hearty dip. The baked toasts add a nice crunch that is no-fat!

Yield: 6 servings

½ pound cooked black beans or a 1-pound can, drained, or dry beans

3 tablespoons extra, extra virgin olive oil

1 small red onion, thinly sliced and separated into rings

3 tablespoons red wine vinegar

2 cloves garlic, minced

2 tablespoons caribe chile (crushed, northern New Mexican)

1 fresh (or dried) bay leaf

½ teaspoon salt

1. To cook the black beans, place them in a stainless steel or other stewing pot that will not become discolored by the beans. Add water to a level of one inch above the top of the beans. Add a ham bone, ½ onion chopped, 1 clove minced garlic, and ½ teaspoon salt. Stew until the water level needs replacing and add 1 cup chicken stock or to just cover the beans. Cook until a bean is soft and smashes when pressed against the side of the pot. Taste and adjust seasonings. Or, open a can of beans and drain well. In a medium-sized non-reactive bowl, combine the remaining ingredients. Add the beans, stirring well.

2. Cover and refrigerate overnight or store up to a week before serving. To serve, place in an earthenware bowl on a coordinating tray and encircle with the toasts.

Tortilla Toasts

6 to 8 10-inch flour tortillas, preferably whole wheat

Preheat the oven to 400°. Using a sharp chef's knife, slice the tortillas into 12 wedges each and place in a single level on a cookie sheet. Sprinkle with a bit of water or spray lightly with an oil spray. Toast in the oven until lightly browned and crisp. Cool on a rack before serving warm with the Black Bean Salsa.

Herb-Basted Grilled Rib Lamb Chops

This is my favorite way with lamb chops! Placing the baste on the chops flavors them and makes them oh so juicy. Preferably, char to rare to medium-rare doneness for maximum flavor and tenderness.

Yield: 6 servings

12 rib lamb chops, sliced 1¹/₂ inches thick
2 tablespoons extra virgin olive oil
2 medium sprigs fresh rosemary leaves, minced,
   or 2 teaspoons dried
3 garlic cloves, finely minced
2 sprigs fresh thyme leaves, minced (1 teaspoon dried)
Several grinds green or black peppercorns
¹/₂ teaspoon lemon zest, minced

1. Trim excess fat off lamb chops, leaving at least ¼ inch fat margin. Combine the remaining ingredients and smooth on both sides of each chop. Place the chops on a cookie sheet and leave them at room temperature for about an hour.

2. Meanwhile preheat the grill to a medium high heat. Adjust the grill to 3 inches above the coals or source of heat. Place the chops on the grill. Grill about 5 to 6 minutes on a side.

3. Serve on warm plates over the Seared Red Chard with Mint Tomatillo Salsa on the side. Place a mound of Roasted Garlicky Mashed Potatoes on the same plate.

❈   ❈   ❈

Seared Red Chard

Swiss chard until recently was little known in some parts of the country. It has a very attractive appearance and a mild flavor that lends itself to many serving variations. Its flavor complements most any meat or poultry—even duck.

Yield: 6 servings

1 1-pound bunch red chard
1 teaspoon olive oil
2 tablespoons balsamic vinegar

1. Rinse the chard very well, allowing some water to remain on the leaves. Slice crosswise in 1-inch slices, stem and all. Preheat the oil in a large, heavy skillet over medium high heat. When it is hot, add the chard and cover. Steam for about 5 minutes.

2. Remove the lid, stir and cook the chard until it is wilted and tender—about 5 more minutes. Sprinkle with the vinegar and toss together. Keep warm until ready to serve under the lamb.

Mint Tomatillo Salsa

Even mint extract works to flavor this toothsome salsa that prettily complements the grilled lamb chops.

Yield: 6 servings

3 cups fresh tomatillos (1½ cups cooked)
1 small fresh jalapeño chile
2 tablespoons fresh mint leaves (or ¼ teaspoon
mint extract)

Cook the tomatillos in just enough water to cover. Puree all the ingredients in the blender. Taste and adjust seasonings, adding salt if desired.

Roasted Garlicky Mashed Potatoes with Wild Mushrooms

This recipe makes a generous amount. You and your guests just might eat all of it! We love these! When leftover, they can be served warmed, cold, or sautéed in patties in butter.

Yield: 6 servings

1 head garlic, roasted
½ ounce wild dried mushrooms, such as shitake or
oyster (if unavailable, sauté 1 cup chopped
button mushrooms in 1 tablespoon butter)
6 pounds russet or golden potatoes, peeled
1 teaspoon salt
3 tablespoons sweet (unsalted) butter, cut into cubes
1 cup warm milk or light cream
Several grinds white pepper

1. Preheat the oven to 400°. Roast the garlic a day or more ahead, brushing the outside skin of the head of garlic with a bit of vegetable or olive oil. Bake covered in a garlic baker or wrapped in foil. When the garlic yields to thumb pressure, it is done.

2. Soak the dried mushrooms in water according to the package directions. Drain and mince when ready to add to the cooked potatoes.

3. About an hour before planning to serve, boil a quart of water with the salt in a heavy 5-quart pan with a close-fitting lid. Cut the potatoes into quarters or sixths, depending on the size of the potatoes. Add to the boiling water and cover.

4. When the potatoes feel soft when pierced with a fork (about 20 minutes), drain. Add the butter, stir, and cover immediately. Cut the root end off the garlic and squeeze the roasted garlic out of the skin with the dull side of a knife blade. Squeeze all of it out, then mince.

5. Heat the milk or cream. Warm the mushrooms in a microwave or saute in butter on top of the range. Mash the potatoes; add about half the milk and the pepper and continue mashing and adding milk until the potatoes are of the desired consistency. Stir in the garlic and mushrooms. Taste and adjust salt and pepper. Keep warm until ready to serve.

Deep Dish Peach Pie

This pie has no crust, making it lower in fat and easier to make—but nonetheless delicious. Instead of a crust, the "pie" has a light cake baked around it.

Yield: 4 servings

*5 fresh peaches, or a 32-ounce package of
    frozen peaches, sliced*
2 tablespoons butter
*1 cup sugar (¹/₂ cup if the peaches are frozen
    in syrup)*
1 egg
¹/₂ cup milk
1 cup flour
1 teaspoon baking powder
1 teaspoon almond extract
1 teaspoon cinnamon
*¹/₂ teaspoon crushed pequin quebrado chile
    (optional)*

1. Butter a deep 9-inch pie plate. Arrange peach slices in the bottom in overlapping circles, starting at the outside edge. (If using frozen peaches, be sure to thaw slightly and remove from the syrup. Discard the syrup or reserve for another use.) Preheat the oven to 350°.

2. Beat the butter until creamy, then slowly add the sugar. Add the egg and milk and beat again. Add half of the flour and the baking powder and mix. Add the other half or the flour and the extract and cinnamon. Mix well. Pour over the peaches. Sprinkle lightly with additional cinnamon and sugar and the pequin quebrado, if using.

3. Bake 35 to 40 minutes or until the cake springs back when pressed with your finger or an inserted toothpick comes out clean with no batter clinging. Peaches should be soft.

Espresso

*Make espresso by using ground espresso style coffee
in your regular coffee maker, if you do not
have an espresso maker.*

Supper for Spring

※

※

Spring signals new beginnings, promising fresh flavors, tempting aromas, and meals as welcome as the new season itself. This supper is a perfect celebration of the long-awaited arrival of spring. What better than a party featuring seasonal foods served up handsomely and easily prepared ahead of time?

A light, creamy, green tomatillo soup is followed by a colorful, vegetable-laden chicken dish accompanied by an unusual and delicious rice salad. Ending the meal is a moist, rich Mexican chocolate cake, topped by a nut-filled, crunchy frosting—an exciting variation on one of America's favorite desserts.

A lot of the preparation can be done hours or even a day or two ahead. The rice is best marinated in advance. The vegetables can be readied hours or a day or so before cooking the chicken. Bake the cake up to two days in advance or just hours before serving—it's good either way. The soup takes just moments and has the freshest flavor if prepared just before serving. I've always liked it best at room temperature, though it can be served either chilled or warmed. Decorate the table with spring's bounty of flowers, and complement them with pastel linens and dinnerware.

MENU PLAN

Day or two before (or early in the day):

    Bake and frost the Texas Frontier Cake.

    Prepare the Rice and Piñon Salad.

    Prepare the vegetables for Juanita's Special Rio Grande Chicken.

One hour or some time before:

    Cook the chicken.

    Prepare the salsa.

    Chill the wine.

    Chill the salad plates and forks.

    Warm the dinner plates.

    Set out the ingredients for Strawberry Margaritas.

    Prepare the Tomatillo-Cilantro Cream Soup and chill if desired.

    Set out the coffeemaker.

At serving time:

    Prepare the Strawberry Margaritas and serve.

    Serve the soup.

    Arrange the Rice and Piñon Salad and serve with the chicken.

    Serve the Texas Frontier Cake with coffee.

Strawberry Margaritas

These luscious, fruity drinks can be made as frosty as you like by adding lots of ice—or they can be made stronger by using less ice. You can also vary the fruit according to what's available. Apricots and peaches are especially good. I generally don't salt the rims for margaritas based on sweet fruits.

Yield: 6 servings

2 ounces freshly squeezed lime juice
¹/₂ cup fresh strawberries
1 ounce triple sec
6 ounces tequila, preferably light
2 cups or more ice

Combine all the ingredients in a blender and process until well mixed. Taste and add sugar or more triple sec if sweeter drinks are desired.

Tomatillo-Cilantro Cream Soup

This outstanding soup requires just moments to prepare, once you have the stock. Make an extra rich stock with pieces from the chicken used in the main dish in this menu: Cut off the extra fatty skin at the back and neck cavities and cook together with the giblets, 1 bay leaf, ¹/₂ teaspoon salt, a generous slice of onion, and 3 black peppercorns.

Yield: 6 servings

1 can (10 ounces) tomatillos with juice
1 cup freshly made rich chicken stock
1¹/₂ cups half-and-half
1 tablespoon chopped cilantro leaves, plus
*   6 perfect leaves for garnish*
¹/₄ teaspoon mild red ground chile

1. Place the tomatillos, chicken stock, half-and-half, and chopped cilantro in a blender jar or food processor. Process on a medium speed until pureed and foamy.

2. Pour into chilled bowls and garnish. Center a cilantro leaf in each bowl and sprinkle with the red chile. Chill, if desired, before serving.

Juanita's Special Rio Grande Chicken

Select a very young spring fryer, not over 2¹/₂ pounds, for this recipe, and the freshest, top-quality vegetables. The dish almost prepares itself once the chicken is browned and the vegetables are prepared. Use a large heavy skillet, a Dutch oven, or even a deep cast-iron pot, as long as it has a tight-fitting cover. You can cook this to the almost-done stage and then heat just before serving, a technique I prefer so that I don't have to watch the clock after my guests have arrived.

Yield: 6 servings

2 tablespoons sweet (unsalted) butter

1 young frying chicken, about 2¹/₂ pounds, cut into serving pieces

3 zucchini, about 1¹/₂ inches in diameter and 6 inches long, cut in ³/₄-inch slices on the bias

4 ears fresh corn kernels cut off the cob, or 2¹/₂ cups frozen, defrosted

2 large, fresh red ripe tomatoes (1 pound each), parched, peeled, and cut into wedges

1 cup thin rounds of small white or yellow Spanish onions

3 garlic cloves, minced

1 jalapeño chile, about 2¹/₂ inches long, chopped

¹/₂ teaspoon cumin

1. Melt the butter over medium heat in a large heavy pot. Add the chicken, skin side down, and turn frequently to brown evenly.

2. When the chicken is browned, add the vegetables in layers—zucchini, corn, tomatoes, and onions. Sprinkle the garlic, jalapeño, and cumin over the top, cover, and steam, reducing heat to just maintain steaming. Check after 30 minutes to be certain all is cooking properly. (If cooking in advance, stop the cooking at this point before the vegetables are completely done.) Then continue to cook for about 30 minutes longer, or until vegetables are done.

3. To serve, place on a platter with the chicken encircled with the vegetables. For added zip and to suit a mixture of palates—from gringos to chile fire-eaters—serve a side dish of *salsa fresca* (see the following recipe). Or add extra chopped jalapeño to the original dish.

❧

Salsa for Pollo

1 jalapeño, about 3 inches long, finely chopped

1 small red ripe tomato, chopped

2 slices (¹/₄ inch thick) red Spanish onion, chopped

Combine and serve in a small bowl with the chicken.

Rice and Piñon Salad

I developed this tasty recipe when looking for a change from the steamed or Mexican rice and tossed salad that so predictably accompany southwestern dinners. Piñons (both the nuts and the tree) are an integral part of northern New Mexico culture—the choice nut for local sweets and confections, a favorite fireplace wood, and the preferred tree for Christmas. However, the trees have recently become increasingly scarce, and as they require centuries to replace, their by-products are not as readily available as they were when I was young. Pine nuts, however, can be purchased as an import, as they are also grown in the Mediterranean (as pignoli) and are used in Italian and Middle Eastern dishes.

Yield: 6 servings

1 cup basmati or long-grain rice
1³/4 cups water
1 teaspoon salt
1 tablespoon sweet (unsalted) butter
6 tablespoons extra virgin olive or salad oil
2 tablespoons cider vinegar
1/4 cup chopped green bell pepper
1/4 cup sliced pimiento-stuffed olives
1/4 cup piñons (pine nuts)
1 head of red leaf lettuce, rinsed and chilled
12 to 18 thin slices of red Spanish onion

1. Combine the rice, water, salt, and butter and bring to a boil. Stir, reduce heat, and cover.

2. Cook 15 minutes over very low heat. Remove cover and fluff with a fork. Set aside while you prepare the dressing.

3. Combine the oil, vinegar, bell pepper, olives, and piñons. Stir into the rice and chill at least 2 hours before serving. Stir once or twice while marinating.

4. To serve, place the lettuce leaves on chilled salad plates. Then heap on the rice salad mixture. Top each serving with the red onion rings. If desired, sprinkle on a few extra piñon nuts.

Texas Frontier Cake

Once known as funeral cake, this dessert was a favorite in the sparsely settled arid regions of West Texas. In the nineteenth century, early settlers rarely got to a grocery store—sometimes as seldom as once a year. Funeral cake, a very simple recipe with a fabulous flavor, could easily be made from ingredients on hand and stored. It also traveled well as its current name implies—in the West, family and friends took (and still do take) large quantities of foods over to the bereaved to help ease the heartache, and this cake was a very popular and delicious offering.

Yield: One 9 x 13-inch loaf

2 cups flour
2 cups sugar
½ pound sweet butter (2 sticks or 1 cup)
⅓ cup cocoa
1 cup water
½ cup buttermilk
2 eggs, slightly beaten
1 teaspoon baking soda
1 teaspoon cinnamon, or more for a spicier taste
1 teaspoon vanilla
Chocolate Icing (recipe follows)

1. Stir together the flour and sugar in a large mixing bowl. Melt the butter with the cocoa and water in a saucepan, bringing to a boil. Pour the hot liquid over the flour mixture and stir well.

2. Add the buttermilk, eggs, baking soda, cinnamon, and vanilla. Beat well and pour into a buttered 9 x 13-inch pan.

3. Bake 30 minutes at 400°, or until the cake springs back when touched.

4. Meanwhile, prepare the icing and spread on the cake while it is still hot.

Note: The cake will stay moist, covered with plastic wrap, for several days.

Chocolate Icing

¼ pound sweet butter
⅓ cup cocoa
⅓ cup milk
1 pound (4⅓ cups) confectioners' sugar
1 teaspoon vanilla
1 cup coarsely chopped pecans

Combine the butter, cocoa, and milk in a 2-quart saucepan. Bring to a boil. Remove from the heat and add the confectioners' sugar. Beat well and stir in the vanilla and nuts. The icing should be medium thick.

Cinco de Mayo

✻

M   E   N   U

Quesadillas Trio

Tequila Sours

Sweet Red Peppered Rice

Roast Loin of Pork en Mole Salsa

Oaxacan Fresh Fruit Salad

Rioja Wine

Tia's Monterrey Flan Flambé

Mexican Coffee

✻

The fifth of May is celebrated in Mexico to commemorate its gaining independence during the Mexican Revolution. This holiday is honored increasingly often in the Southwest as well as all over the United States. Cinco de Mayo gives everyone the opportunity to have a huge fiesta and to enjoy the mariachi music and all the color and trimmings that can be conjured. Serve this dinner every May 5 for lots of fun and luck!

The entire menu for this meal is based on traditional dishes—with some innovative touches. The *quesadillas*, prepared in a trio of flavors, are actually inside-out nachos, whose filling is blanketed with a grilled wheat tortilla. In addition to the traditional cheese and jalapeño filling, I have developed *chorizo*-sour cream and avocado-chicken versions. All are laced with guacamole and garnished with cilantro. Served with Tequila Sours, which are quite popular in Mexico, they make a super introduction to this celebration dinner.

The *mole*, a rich brown, well-flavored sauce, gently permeates the pork tenderloin. Because of the firmer texture of the pork, as opposed to the more often used turkey or chicken, the flavoring of the meat is quite subtle. For those who wish a stronger flavor, serve the sauce alongside for spooning over the pork and rice.

Sweet red peppers and vegetables punctuate the rice accompaniment, adding an explosion of color and a richer flavor that perfectly complements the *mole*.

The Oaxacan Fresh Fruit Salad was inspired by my visits with my uncle and Mexican aunt, whose favorite city was Oaxaca. It is a beautiful, historic, and picturesque place nestled in the mountains south of Mexico City, where its citizens enjoy the bounty of the tropics in a high-altitude climate.

The flan, which is my aunt's recipe, is a glorious finale!

Stage this meal with color and verve. Create a definite Mexican atmosphere with lots of brightly colored flowers—either real or paper—in tall urns or baskets. Use red, green, and white with other bright accents in the table linens. Be sure to have mariachi music, even if it's on tape.

MENU PLAN

Day before (or earlier):
   Prepare the flan and chill.
   Prepare the salad dressing.

Early in the day (or the day before):
   Marinate the pork loin in the *mole* sauce

Three hours before:
   Cook the pork loin; let stand 30 minutes
      before carving.
   Prepare the salad fruits.
   Prepare the vegetables for the rice; cook the
      rice just before the guests arrive.
   Prepare the *quesadillas*; grill them about
      30 minutes before the guests arrive.

   Warm the dinner plates and chill the
      salad plates and forks.
   Make the guacamole.
   Make the Tequila Sours.
   Set up the coffeepot.

At serving time:
   Cut the quesadillas into sixths and garnish.
      Serve with the Tequila Sours.
   Carve the pork and dress the salad. Serve
      with the rice.
   While the guests are eating, heat the flan
      and make the coffee.
   Serve the flaming flan at the table.
   Serve the coffee.

Quesadillas Trio

Quesadillas *are wheat tortillas folded over an oozing blend of Monterey Jack cheese spiked with hot, hot jalapeños, then quickly grilled on a lightly buttered* tapa *or* comal *(a Mexican or Spanish griddle).*

For this celebratory dinner I have developed some delicious alternatives to this southwestern standard. Try serving chorizo *(Mexican style sausage) with sour cream and chicken with avocado and green chiles in addition to the traditional cheese and chile combination. Serve with your favorite salsa, if desired.*

Yield: 6 servings

1 to 2 tablespoons sweet (unsalted) butter, melted
6 freshly made 10-inch wheat tortillas
3 cups grated Monterey Jack and cheddar cheese,
  combined or 1½ cups each
¼ cup pickled or fresh jalapeño slices, or to taste
2 chorizo sausages, fried, drained, and crumbled
½ cup chopped, cooked chicken
1 tablespoon or more chopped hot New Mexico
  green chiles
½ ripe avocado, cut in long thin slivers
Sour cream if desired
Bunch of fresh cilantro, rinsed
1 small tomato coarsely chopped
1 cup salsa, your choice, if desired
1 tablespoon caribe chile

1. Melt the butter and lightly brush two preheated griddles heated to medium high heat. Brush butter in the shape of one half a tortilla and place one half of the tortilla over the butter. Sprinkle that half with a layer of ½ cup of the cheese and then with a few jalapeño slices. Fold the top half of the tortilla over the filling and grill the first side until golden. Brush the top side of the tortilla with a bit of melted butter and turn to brown the second side. Remove to a cutting board. Make two of these.

2. Butter pan as above. On each of two tortillas, place ½ cup cheese, then sprinkle on ½ the crumbled chorizo and a few jalapeño slices. Cook as above. On each of the remaining two tortillas, place a layer of the ½ cup cheese, half the chicken, then evenly sprinkle with the hot green chile and avocado slivers.

3. Grill first sides of the tortillas until golden. Fold down top sides, brush with butter, and turn. Grill second sides. Remove to cutting board.

4. To serve, cut each into thirds. Place them on an oversized Mexican or earthenware platter. Center a dollop of sour cream or salsa on each at the tip ends and nestle a bunch of cilantro around the crust edge. Sprinkle with tomato pieces, and scatter caribe like confetti over all.

Note: Fresh chopped tomato and onion can be added to the chorizo quesadillas. Other fillings can be used.

Tequila Sours

For ages, these have had a following in Mexico as well as along the border, where many bartenders have learned to make very good versions. This variation is easy to prepare for a crowd and is quite good.

Yield: 6 drinks

1 can (6 ounces) frozen lemonade concentrate
1¹⁄₃ cups light tequila
12 or more ice cubes
6 orange slices, rind and all
6 maraschino cherries

1. Using a blender, place the lemonade, tequila, and 6 ice cubes in the jar and process on high speed until well mixed. Add 6 more cubes and blend until slushy. If not slushy enough, keep adding ice cubes and processing.
2. Serve in goblets, with a slice of orange curled over the rim of the glass and a cherry attached with a toothpick.

Sweet Red Peppered Rice

This pretty, vegetable-flavored rice is an essential accompaniment to the mole, as it allows the rich sauce to be fully savored.

Yield: 6 servings

2 tablespoons sweet (unsalted) butter
1 large fresh red sweet pepper, cut into ³⁄₄-inch dice
³⁄₄ cup finely diced carrot
³⁄₄ cup finely diced celery
³⁄₄ cup finely diced Spanish onion
1¹⁄₂ cups long grain rice
3 cups chicken stock
1 teaspoon salt, or to taste (depends on seasoning in broth)
3 tablespoons chopped flat-leaf parsley

1. Melt the sweet butter in a heavy 3-quart saucepan, then add the vegetables and rice and lightly sauté, until all are coated with butter.
2. Add the chicken stock and bring to a boil; reduce the heat to a simmer, cover, and cook for 15 minutes. Do not peek. When the time is up, stir, add salt, and replace the cover, ajar, to keep it warm and allow the rice to fluff. To serve, remove the cover and sprinkle the rice with parsley.

Roast Loin of Pork en Mole Salsa

Mole *is unquestionably the national dish of Mexico, so it is an obvious choice for this celebratory dinner. The only adaptation I've made is to use pork instead of the more traditional turkey or chicken. The ancient origins of mole are lost in the mists of time, but its popularity as a festive dish stems from the seventeenth century, when the nuns of the Santa Rosa convent used it either (historians differ) to celebrate their release from captivity or as thanks to the archbishop for building them a grand convent.*

The variations for the sauce are endless, but the key ingredients are always the same for poblano mole, *the classic version: a blend of chiles, chocolate, and spices with varying quantities of nuts, tortillas, tomatoes, and other additions. Mole is now available in a powder or concentrate, which I've used in this recipe. I've found that the Doña Maria brand in an 8¼-ounce glass jar is quite good. It is regularly imported from Mexico and available in specialty stores.*

This dish requires marination for most of a day or overnight.

Yield: 6 servings

3 to 4 pounds of pork loin
8¼ ounces mole concentrate
1¼ cups water
2 large garlic cloves, minced

1. Clean and trim the pork, removing excess fat but leaving a thin blanket of fat around the exterior. Put in a large shallow glass baking dish.

2. Remove the *mole* paste from the jar and place in a small mixing bowl. Stir in 1¼ cups warm water and the garlic and mix well. Drizzle over the pork, turning it to coat the entire roast evenly. Spoon the sauce over the roast every 15 minutes and rotate frequently. Leave covered at room temperature for at least 2 hours, or refrigerate overnight.*

3. Roast in a 325° oven, basting frequently, for 3 hours. Allow to cool at least 30 minutes before carving. Serve with a side dish of the sauce, which is terrific over the rice.

Note: Leaving pork at room temperature for two hours is safe so long as it has been refrigerated prior to preparation.

Oaxacan Fresh Fruit Salad

The influence is clear here—this salad contains the tropical fruits of Mexico and is laced with a favorite dressing I've been making since I was a kid. The colors are festive and follow the Mexican custom of always decorating at least one dish with the national colors—red, white, and green.

Yield: 6 servings

1/2 Mexican pineapple, peeled, cored, and cut into wedges
1 papaya, preferably watermelon pink, peeled, seeded, and cut into squares
2 cups watermelon balls
Honey Poppy Seed Dressing (recipe follows)
2 Haas avocados, cut into long thin strips
1 pomegranate
1 head red leaf lettuce, rinsed well and blotted dry

1. Cut all the fruit as directed and combine all but the avocado and pomegranate.
2. Prepare the salad dressing.
3. Add the dressing to the combined fruit mixture and gently toss. Then arrange the lettuce leaves on chilled salad plates. Spoon the salad onto the lettuce and garnish with the wedges of avocado, spooning any dressing remaining in the salad bowl over the avocado. Peel the pomegranate, carefully pick out the red seeds, and sprinkle them over each salad.

Honey Poppy Seed Dressing

Yield: 1 1/2 cups

3/4 cup fragrant blossom honey
1 teaspoon salt
1 teaspoon dry mustard
1/3 cup white wine vinegar
1 1/2 tablespoons chopped onion
1 1/2 tablespoons poppy seeds
1 cup soy or peanut oil

Place all the ingredients in a blender jar or food processor and process until blended. Keep at room temperature until ready to use. Reserve any left in a covered jar in the refrigerator. Keeps well.

Tia's Monterrey Flan Flambé

My aunt from Monterrey, Mexico, was a fabulous cook, and this was one of her favorite desserts—which she prepared as an excuse for celebrating almost anything! Served flaming, it's most impressive, yet quite easily done. Make this a day or more ahead and chill before warming to serve.

Yield: 6 servings

¾ cup granulated sugar
1 tablespoon sweet (unsalted) butter
1¼ cups coarsely chopped pecans
15 ounces sweetened condensed milk
15 ounces milk, rinsed in the condensed milk can
6 eggs
1 teaspoon Mexican vanilla, or pure vanilla extract
1 cup 80-proof light rum

1. Caramelize ½ cup of the sugar in a heavy skillet over medium high heat, stirring constantly with a wooden spoon. While it is still hot and syrupy, pour over the bottom of a buttered 1½-quart mold or baking dish.

2. Immediately sprinkle the pecans uniformly over the sugar.

3. In an electric blender, food processor, or mixer, combine the milks, eggs, and vanilla and whip until foamy. Slowly pour over the caramelized sugar.

4. Place the mold or baking dish in another larger pan to which an inch or more of water has been added to create a water bath. Bake at 350° for 1 hour, or until a knife inserted in the center comes out clean. Chill in refrigerator to develop the caramelized syrup.

5. To serve, reheat at 300° in the mold until a knife inserted allows steam to escape. Unmold on a warm plate, preferably silver. Carefully warm the rum over medium low heat, watching for the very first bubble. Immediately sprinkle the top of the flan with the remaining ¼ cup sugar. Dim the lights, pour the rum over the top and ignite, and present the flan at the table.

Mexican Coffee

Serve a good, dark roast Mexican arabica coffee, carefully brewed.

Early June Dinner

✤

M   E   N   U

Frozen Lime Daiquiris

Chilled Tomato-Cilantro Soup

Soft-Shell Crabs with Jalapeño Salsa

New Mexican Pesto and Cappellini

Fresh Strawberries with Cointreau Cream

Pinot Chardonnay

Coffee

✤

When the crickets begin to hum and your heart turns to an early summer menu to perk up winter-hardened appetites, consider this meal—with flavors as fresh as early June flowers.

Innovation is the keynote to this menu. The bright, clear, springlike color and flavor of the daiquiris provide an ideal opener to whet appetites in this pastel setting. The light, subtle tang of the Tomato-Cilantro Soup, followed by delicate soft-shell crabs laced with hot spicy salsa, make for a wonderfully balanced meal. Be sure to select the tiniest, freshest, softest soft-shell crabs you can find. Steer away from those with papery shells and the harder, larger, crustier crabs—they are not nearly as fine.

Serve a New Mexican Pesto with pasta as an accompaniment—its hot green chile adds a welcome piquancy to the fragrant basil. And to follow, what could be a finer treat for stroking and soothing the palate than a pillow of whipped cream with tangy bitter orange cradling luscious red ripe strawberries?

Serve this dinner either in your dining room, on a porch or patio, or in the garden. The table will be prettiest if you decorate it in pinks and softest greens. Lacking regular linens in these shades, you can improvise with ginghams or other fabrics from a yard goods store, or look through your scarves or bed linens. Even an accent of pink and lime green satin ribbon on white or natural lace or linen would be nice. Flowers are a must for so special a salute to the beginning of wonderful outdoor times! Arrange huge garden bouquets for the side tables, if serving indoors, and create a smaller, lower level one for the centerpiece.

MENU PLAN

Day before (or early in the day):

Prepare the tomato-cilantro soup and chill.
Prepare the Jalapeño Salsa and chill.
Prepare the New Mexican Pesto and chill.
Prepare the Cointreau Cream and chill.
Chill a dry white wine such as Pinot Chardonnay or Blanc de Blanc.

Two hours before:

Rinse, hull, and sugar the strawberries.
Set out the pot for the pasta, filling it with salted, oiled water.
Place the soup bowls and the goblets for both the daiquiris and the strawberries in the freezer.
Make the Frozen Lime Daiquiris.

At serving time:

Serve the daiquiris.
Lightly sauté the crabs just before serving the soup, and set aside.
Heat the dinner plates.
Boil the water and carefully cook the pasta to the *al dente* stage while you are serving and clearing the soup.
Toss the pasta with the pesto and serve with the crabs.
Arrange the strawberries in the cream in the chilled goblets just before serving.

Frozen Lime Daiquiris

These spring-green, refreshing drinks key in perfectly with this dinner. And like all rum drinks, they always seem to promise beaches, seafood, and all the wonderful pleasures of summer.

Yield: 6 drinks

1 can (6 ounces) frozen limeade
1¹/₃ cups light rum
12 or more ice cubes
6 thin rounds of fresh lime
6 sprigs of fresh mint

1. Place the limeade, rum, and about half the ice in a blender jar and process until the ice is crushed. Continue adding ice until the desired consistency is reached.

2. Serve in tall, chilled globe-shaped goblets, garnishing each with a thin slice of lime and a sprig of mint.

❈   ❈   ❈

Chilled Tomato-Cilantro Soup

Somewhat reminiscent of a pureed gazpacho, this delightfully light, mildly spicy soup features the brisk, clean taste of cilantro. The flavors marry best when the soup is prepared a day or at least a few hours in advance.

Yield: 6 servings

2 tablespoons virgin olive oil
1 large Spanish onion, coarsely chopped in a
*   food processor*
1 large carrot, scraped and coarsely chopped
*   in a food processor*
1 can (28 ounces) whole tomatoes, coarsely
*   chopped in a food processor*
¹/₂ teaspoon caribe (or other crushed dried red chile)
1 can (4 ounces) green chiles
¹/₄ cup fresh cilantro (reserve 6 whole leaves for
*   garnish)*

1. Place the olive oil in a heavy 2-quart saucepan. Add the onion and carrot and cook about 4 minutes, stirring frequently.

2. Add the tomatoes and caribe and cook for 10 minutes more.

3. Place the mixture in a food processor and process with the green chiles and cilantro until pureed.

4. Chill the soup and serve in chilled soup bowls, garnishing each with a cilantro leaf.

Soft-Shell Crabs with Jalapeño Salsa

Soft-shell crabs—once nearly impossible to get in New Mexico and throughout most of the Southwest—are now more easily available, and are a treat for spring and early summer. Although I am very fond of them prepared in almost any fashion—including simply sautéed with fresh lemon, butter, and parsley—this recipe is perhaps my favorite. Be very selective when you shop for crabs. Check to see that they are alive and that their skins are greenish, very soft, and fresh looking. Papery shells make for less pleasurable eating. I've specified tiny ones for the menu, as I find the larger crabs, combined with the pesto, make for too heavy a meal. If only medium-sized ones are available, you may wish to serve just one to a diner.

Yield: 6 servings

¼ pound sweet (unsalted) butter
12 tiny soft-shell crabs, cleaned (see Note below)
½ cup or more flour
Salt and freshly ground black pepper to taste
1 fresh lime, cut into six long wedges
6 sprigs of cilantro
Jalapeño Salsa, chilled

1. Melt the butter in a large skillet. Lightly dust each crab with the flour. Sauté over medium heat, turning when the first side becomes golden. Sprinkle lightly with salt and pepper.

2. When the crabs are done—they are golden brown —place them on hot plates and pour the pan juices over them. Garnish with lime, cilantro, and a ribbon of Jalapeño Salsa. (Follow the Salsa Fresca recipe on page 33, substituting 4 to 6 deveined, seeded and very finely chopped fresh jalapeños for the diced chiles. It's not necessary to parch and peel them.)

Note: Prepare live crabs as follows: Cut off the apron or flap that folds under the rear of the body. Turn the crab over and cut off the face at a joint just back of the eyes. Lift each point at the sides with the fingers and clean out the gills. Wash crabs with cold water and pat dry with paper towels.

New Mexican Pesto and Cappellini

Create this flavorful pesto whenever you can lay your hands on fresh basil. It can be served right after making or frozen whenever basil is most bountiful. Basil is an aromatic annual and is just wonderful this way. I make dozens of jars of pesto different ways in late summer in my Corrales kitchen, then freeze it to enjoy during the winter and spring. The New Mexican touch is the addition of fresh green chiles, which produce just the right pizzazz. If you have a batch of ready-made pesto, you can process it with the right amount of green chile in the food processor. For another variation, substitute an equal amount of fresh cilantro for the fresh basil.

Yield: 6 servings

*2 cups fresh basil leaves, rinsed, torn, and
  packed together*
1/2 cup virgin olive oil
3 tablespoons piñons (pine nuts)
2 large garlic cloves
1/4 teaspoon salt, or to taste
*1/2 cup finely chopped New Mexican green chiles,
  freshly parched and peeled (see page 17),
  or canned or frozen*
1/2 cup freshly grated Parmesan cheese
3 tablespoons grated Romano cheese
*3 tablespoons sweet butter, softened to room
  temperature*
*12 ounces cappellini/angel hair pasta
  (very fine spaghetti)*
1 tablespoon salt
2 tablespoons olive oil

1. Rinse, sort, and tear the basil into small pieces and pack, pressing firmly yet lightly enough so as not to crush the delicate leaves.

2. Place the leaves, oil, piñon nuts, garlic, and salt in a food processor or electric blender. Process only until pureed, being careful not to overprocess.

3. Pour into a 1-quart mixing bowl and add the green chile and cheeses. Stir until evenly mixed. Stir in the softened butter and combine well. Add one or two tablespoons of the pasta-cooking water while it is cooking.

4. Prepare the pasta, boiling it in 5 quarts water with 1 tablespoon salt and 2 tablespoons olive oil. Cook only until *al dente*—about 4 minutes in rapidly boiling water. Rinse with hot water, drain, and toss with the pesto. Serve alongside the crabs with salsa.

Fresh Strawberries with Cointreau Cream

What single food announces June and the coming summer as satisfyingly as strawberries? I remember so well the painful pleasures of hours and hours of backbreaking work picking berries in the earthy heat of the strawberry beds. Somehow the rewards of popping occasional berries, warm and juicy, into one's mouth, and the anticipation of the many tasty treats to be made from the berries always kept us going. Freshly picked vine-ripened berries are always the best, and well worth the ride to the fields if you are a city dweller. If you have to buy them from a grocer, though, be sure to select very ripe, firm berries for this dish.

Yield: 6 servings

1 quart red ripe strawberries
1 cup confectioners' sugar
1 cup vanilla ice cream
1 cup heavy whipping cream
1/3 cup Cointreau or other orange-flavored brandy

1. Carefully rinse the berries and select only the firm ripe ones. Hull and leave whole. Layer with 1/2 cup confectioners' sugar generously sprinkled over them. Gently toss to coat evenly. Allow to set at room temperature at least 2 hours.

2. Soften the ice cream so that it can be beaten with a whisk. Whip the cream in a well-chilled bowl using high speed on the mixer. Once the cream begins to foam, add the remaining 1/2 cup sugar and continue beating until very stiff. Fold in the ice cream and Cointreau. Taste and adjust flavoring.

3. Serve in well-chilled crystal goblets (place in freezer before serving the meal), arranging the strawberries in layers with the whipped cream mixture. Top each serving with a perfect berry.

III ❈ Summer

Sunday Summer Patio Brunch

A Native American Feast to
  Celebrate Indian Market

Summer Garden's Bounty,
  A Vegetarian's Pleasure

Hot Summer Special

Festive Formal Dinner for Four

Sunday Summer Patio Brunch

❧

M E N U

Bloody Marias

Fruit Tostados Compuestas

Chile-Corn Custard Cazuelas

*Navajo Fry Bread with
Homemade Apricot Jam
and Sweet Butter topped with
Freshly Grated Nutmeg*

Mexican Cinnamon Coffee

❧

This colorful New Mexican or Arizonian brunch is intended for a lazy summer weekend when you have time to enjoy preparing these foods. If you make the tostado shells and the jam a day or so ahead, you can easily create the rest of the foods within 2 hours.

The eye-openers, an adaptation of the familiar Bloody Marys, are especially attractive served with a curled cucumber garnish. Another departure from the traditional are the brilliantly colored, perfectly ripe fruits cut in various shapes and served in tostado baskets, which are guaranteed to bring compliments from your guests. The Chile-Corn Custard *Cazuelas* were developed from the favorite local green chiles and are a pleasure both to serve and eat. Navajo Fry Bread, a delicious southwestern classic, can also be used as the basis for Navajo tacos: Just place taco fillings on top of the freshly fried disks of bread.

I recommend serving this meal on the patio, terrace, or deck, or in any other outdoor setting. Decorate the table and dining area with large, old-fashioned bouquets of field or garden flowers, such as daisies, zinnias, gladioli, and dahlias.

MENU PLAN

Day before:

Fry the tostado baskets.
Make the jam.

Two hours before:

Prepare the Bloody Marias mixture and
cucumber garnish. Salt the rims of the
glasses and place in the freezer.
Place the butter in a crockery bowl and
smooth off the top. Chill.
Prepare the fruits for the tostados, gently stir
in the dressing, and chill.
Combine the ingredients for the Navajo Fry
Bread and knead. Set the dough aside. Heat
the oil.

Prepare the Chile-Corn Custard *Cazuelas*
and bake; keep warm in a 150° oven.
Set out the coffeepot.

At serving time:

Garnish the Bloody Marias and serve.
Warm the tostados, fill with fruit, and serve
immediately.
Serve the Chile-Corn Custard *Cazuelas*.
Fry the Navajo Fry Bread. Serve with the jam,
butter, and freshly grated nutmeg.
Brew the coffee and serve.

Bloody Marias

When I first started serving this Albuquerque adaptation of the favorite brunch drink, I found that most of my guests preferred it to the classic Bloody Mary. Serve Bloody Marias in large, heavy Mexican glass goblets or tumblers, or other large tall glasses. An hour or so ahead, frost the glasses in the freezer, adding a salty rim as you would for margaritas. Include a generous garnish—I prefer the curled cucumber stick, as described.

Yield: 12 drinks

2 cans (46 ounces each) good-quality tomato juice
¼ cup Worcestershire sauce
2 tablespoons pickled jalapeño juice, or more to taste
¼ cup hot salsa, optional
1 large dark green cucumber, unpeeled
2 large or 3 small limes, cut into 12 wedges
About 1 teaspoon caribe (or other crushed dried red chile)
1 fifth good-quality natural blue agave tequila, 80 proof or better

1. Salt the rims of the glasses as directed on page 98 in the Perfect Margaritas recipe and freeze.

2. Combine the tomato juice, Worcestershire sauce, jalapeño juice, and salsa in a large pitcher. This can be done hours ahead if desired.

3. Prepare the garnish. Using a very sharp knife, slice the cucumber lengthwise, then cut lengthwise again into quarters, then cut each quarter into thirds to create 12 long wedges. Using the point of your knife, carefully pull back the peel about halfway up the length of the cucumber wedge. Soak in ice water, if time permits. This should help the cucumber peeling to curl. Just before preparing the drinks, cut one lime in half or use the cut lime you used for juicing the rims of the glasses. Squeeze a dribble of the juice down the tops of each wedge of cucumber. For a pretty effect, lightly dust each cucumber wedge with caribe by placing the caribe on a piece of wax paper and pressing the tops of the cucumber wedges into it. Sometimes I've added a sprinkle of kosher salt.

4. To serve, place three or four ice cubes in each glass. Add 2 ounces of tequila and about 1 cup of the spicy tomato juice mixture to each. Stir each and garnish with a wedge of fresh lime (squeeze it just before adding) to float on the surface. Before serving, attach the cucumber wedge to the rim of each glass with the curled peel hanging over the rim.

Fruit Tostados Compuestos

A beautiful and innovative way to serve fresh summer fruits, these tostado baskets (compuestos) are always a big hit. The crisp bites of tostado are an ideal complement to the meltingly soft flavor of summer fruits.

Yield: 12 servings

2 quarts vegetable oil

1 dozen 10-inch wheat tortillas

12 cups fresh summer fruits in a variety of colors, shapes, and sizes (such as melon balls, strawberries, blueberries, pineapple wedges, and banana rounds)

¼ cup cactus honey or strong-flavored blossom honey

¼ cup freshly squeezed lime juice

1. Heat the oil to 375° in an electric deep-fat fryer or in a deep heavy pot, using a thermometer to maintain the correct temperature.

2. Fry the tortillas, using the *compuesta* technique described on page 22. Drain the fried tostado shells on layers of absorbent paper toweling.

3. Prepare the fruit and place all together in a large bowl. Combine the honey and lime juice. Pour over the fruit and carefully stir to coat the fruit; do not bruise it. Chill until just ready to serve. You can let it marinate up to 2 hours, but not more, as the fruits will start to weep.

4. Warm the tostado baskets in a 250° oven for 10 to 15 minutes, or until warm and crisp (if fried ahead). To serve, place the marinated fruits in the tostado baskets. Try to spoon the fruits in carefully, and artistically arrange the top of each basket. Evenly distribute the juice. Serve immediately.

Chile-Corn Custard Cazuelas

The green chiles in this recipe form a lovely and unusual crust for the golden custard. For greatest flair, prepare in and serve in earthenware bowls (cazuelas).

Yield: 12 servings

2 dozen whole large, fresh New Mexican green chiles, parched (see page 17) and sliced open

6 eggs, beaten

4 cans (15 ounces each) yellow cream-style corn

1½ cups yellow cornmeal (if desired, crumbled tostado or taco shells may be substituted)

1½ teaspoons salt (reduce amount if using salted tostados)

2 garlic cloves, minced

1 teaspoon baking powder

12 tablespoons sweet butter, melted

2 cups grated sharp cheddar cheese (not necessary to grate if using a food processor or blender; can use low or no-fat cheddar or Jack cheese to reduce fat)

1. Butter 12 ovenproof earthenware bowls or individual casseroles. Then peel the chiles, remove the stems, and rinse out the seeds, leaving the chiles whole. Place two whole, sliced open chiles in each casserole, big or stem end up, slightly above the rim of each bowl. As uniformly as possible, stretch the two chiles to cover the bottom and sides of each.

2. Place all the remaining ingredients in a food processor or blender and process until well blended.

3. Pour into the individual, green chile-lined casseroles, dividing the mixture evenly. Bake 30 minutes at 375°, then reduce the temperature to 325° for another 10 minutes, or until an inserted knife comes out clean. These keep amazingly well. I've kept them in a 150° oven for 3 or 4 hours while awaiting serving time and they really do not suffer. Place the casserole dishes on a service plate to serve.

Navajo Fry Bread

This historic bread is always a treat and can be served in many different ways. For this menu, I recommend serving it freshly fried. In fact, you can even get your friends involved. Many people who appreciate southwestern food—or just have a curiosity and a healthy appetite—enjoy learning how to make this bread, as they do sopaipillas.

I've always believed that sopaipillas were derived from Navajo Fry Bread, for while the frying technique is different, the dough is nearly the same. Sopaipillas are squares of deep-fried dough that puff and become hollow, whereas this bread is fried in large disks. To keep it from becoming one huge puff, holes are poked into the dough after it has been rolled. Traditionally it is cooked on the end of a green piñon twig by Navajo women and is a major attraction at fairs, festivals, rodeos, horse shows, and other local events in the New Mexico/Arizona area. With gorgeous turquoise dripping about their wrists and necks, the Navajo women fry the breads in a big cast-iron pot of lard, heated over an open piñon fire. Just the memory makes me yearn for some!

Yield: 24 medium disks

2 or more quarts vegetable oil (or lard if you
    want to be traditional)
4 cups all-purpose flour, carefully measured*
1 tablespoon plus 2 teaspoons baking powder
1 teaspoon salt
1 tablespoon lard or butter
1 1/3 cups warm water, approximately
Additional flour
Cornmeal and/or herbs, optional

*Note: When measuring flour, spoon it into a dry measure and carefully level it off—otherwise you will get too much flour and a poor product.

1. Heat the oil to 375° in an electric deep-fat fryer or deep cooking pot. Use a deep-fat thermometer to maintain the proper temperature if you do not have the fryer.

2. Mix the flour with baking powder and salt. Work in the lard or butter with a pastry blender or a fork. Add about ½ cup of the water. Mix and stir, then add water until a very stiff but cohesive dough results. The consistency should be like bread dough. When punched, it should be very firm. Knead it generously to gain a very smooth dough.

3. Let it rest about 10 minutes, covered. Then pull off small balls of dough, 2 to 3 inches in diameter. Flatten each ball and form into a circle by overlapping the edges as you would to seal a double-crust pie pastry. Sprinkle additional flour on the board, being careful to add only a light dusting. Roll and turn with a small rolling pin (in New Mexico, it's called a *bolillo*, usually 8 inches long and 2 inches in diameter), creating even pressure as you roll. Once rolled to a thickness of ¼ inch, add cornmeal, crushed herbs, even juniper berries for a traditional, yet novel, taste and texture, if desired. Using a large meat fork, pierce 4 to 6 holes, with a predominant one in the center of the disk.

4. Fry one at a time, watching carefully. If they start to puff, immediately pierce deeper holes. Use tongs to turn as soon as one side becomes golden.

5. Drain each on absorbent paper toweling. Keep warm in a low oven while you fry the remaining disks. Serve warm with cinnamon-sugar, honey, or preserves.

Homemade Apricot Jam

Apricot trees grow easily and bear abundantly in Albuquerque and throughout New Mexico, all along the river valleys. We had a favorite tree in our backyard, which brings back memories of the wondrous, perfume flavor of freshly made jam.

The jam was a perfect way of using windfall crops—being certain to use mostly underripe fruit, with some overripe to create the best texture and flavor. If you prefer jam that retains the shape of the fruit, allow the sugared fruit to stand overnight, or at least for a few hours. If your preference is for a pureed consistency, then begin to prepare the jam immediately after preparing the fruit, mashing it as it cooks.

Yield: 6 jars

3 cups apricots, halved, pits removed
2½ cups granulated sugar

1. Prepare the fruit. Depending on the preferred consistency, let it set with the sugar or proceed immediately.

2. Mix the sugar very well with the apricots in a large heavy saucepan.

3. Place over medium-high heat and bring to a boil, then reduce the heat somewhat to maintain a boil, yet not scorch. Cook and stir frequently until it reaches 7° above the boiling point at whatever altitude you are (219° at sea level). To test for doneness, hold a spoon upright in the jam, then lift it straight up, allowing the drops of jam to "sheet off."

4. Meanwhile, scrub the jelly jars and place them in a large shallow pan. Add an inch of water and boil for 5 minutes to sterilize the jars.

5. Once the jam is done, set aside on the counter to cool slightly. Skim the foam from the surface and top sides of the pan. Then place the still warm jam in the sterilized jars. Seal and cool away from drafts, or seal with melted paraffin after the jam has cooled.

Mexican Cinnamon Coffee

Mexican coffee has many interpretations. Restaurants often serve it with liqueurs and multicolored whipped cream. Following a rather heavy meal, I prefer the simplicity of a good, dark roast Mexican arabica coffee, carefully brewed. You can use any favorite dark roasted coffee. For greatest flavor, freshly grind your coffee and brew it with a hint of cinnamon. For 12 cups or more, the quantity for this brunch, use about 1 1/2 teaspoons cinnamon sprinkled over the grounds.

Later in the day you can also serve Kahlúa or brandy on the side.

Yield: 12 cups

3/4 to 1 cup freshly ground dark roast Mexican arabica coffee or enough to brew 12 cups of strong, full-flavored coffee

1 1/2 teaspoons ground cinnamon

1 cup heavy whipping cream

1/2 teaspoon Mexican vanilla, if available, or 1 teaspoon pure vanilla extract

1/4 cup sugar

12 cinnamon sticks, each 4 inches long

Raw natural sugar crystals (piloncillo)

1. Place the ground coffee in the drip basket, or wherever grounds are held in your pot. Add the ground cinnamon. Brew the coffee.

2. Meanwhile, prepare the whipped cream, adding the vanilla and sugar as it whips. Whip to a firm consistency, with stiff peaks.

3. Serve the coffee in mugs—heavy Mexican pottery would be perfect. Add a cinnamon stick to each and serve with the whipped cream and *piloncillo*.

Note: *Piloncillo* is raw sugar in Old Mexico. It is often formed into hard cones.

A Native American Feast to Celebrate Indian Market

❧

M E N U

Firewater Spritzers

Herbed Sun Mint Tea

Sage Bread Toasts
with Fresh Tomato Salsa

Navajo Tacos

Roasted Baby Blue or Red Potato Salad

Black Mesa Apricot Crumble

❧

Santa Fe's Indian Market is very festive. Stemming from the fiestas celebrated for centuries, the market has evolved into a gathering place for Native American artists of all kinds. Indians come not only from the Southwest but also from Alaska to Florida to display their beautiful works of art—from fine sculpture to jewelry, clothing, and wall hangings. Afficionados who value beauty and quality come from all over the world to this event. Many, once they have attended, return year after year.

Parties are an ongoing tradition during Indian Market. Certain families always hold their events at exactly the same time, year after year, devoting a great deal of thought to just how to make their luncheons and dinners distinctive.

With all this background in mind, I created a luncheon that you could host most any time or place. Of course Santa Fe during Indian Market in August is the most special, but you can transport yourself there with this menu—a true fiesta!

Do use your southwestern Indian fabrics, dishes, and art if you have them. If you don't, they are easy to find. The fabrics and even the everyday pottery abound, nationwide. If you are fond of this theme, why not select some fabric or weaving you like and continue using it afterwards. The same with the dishes—you will get lots of pleasure from them. An Indian blanket, colorful burlap, or an Indian red, black, or turquoise linen tablecloth will also create a pleasing background. Straw baskets with colorful napkins add to the effect. Tall vases with dried grass can grace a buffet table, and for a sit-down meal, a centerpiece of straw flowers will go nicely. For a late summer luncheon, cut garden flowers are beautiful.

MENU PLAN

Day before (or earlier):
   Make plum nectar, if you cannot buy it.
   Bake the apricot crumble (it can be frozen).
   Bake the sage bread (it can also be frozen).
   Roast the potatoes the day before and make
      the potato salad.

Early in the day:
   Prepare the Navajo Taco dough.
   Prepare the toppings for the Navajo Tacos.
   Make the tea.

One hour before:
   Heat the oil and fry the bread for the
      Navajo Tacos. Keep warm.

   Prepare the tomato salsa.
   Prepare the garnish for drinks.
   Warm the apricot crumble, if made ahead,
      in 200° oven.
   Warm the sage bread in 200° oven along
      with the dinner plates.

At serving time:
   Serve the Firewater Spritzers.
   Serve the sage bread with the Fresh Tomato
      Salsa.
   Serve the Navajo Tacos with the potato salad
      and iced sun tea.
   Serve the apricot crumble.

Firewater Spritzers

These are thirst quenching and fun, and the plums add a different and delightful flavor! Southwest Native Americans are very fond of wild plums and use them or wild cherries to flavor many delicacies.

Yield: 6 servings

3 cups wild or Santa Rosa plum nectar (see step #1)
½ cup granulated sugar or to taste
6 shots vodka (1 ounce each)
1 quart seltzer water
2 fresh wild or Santa Rosa plums, pitted and cut in 6 wedges for garnish

1. Prepare the nectar by stewing at least 2 pounds plums, halved and seeds removed, with water to cover. Stew until soft, then strain through a fine sieve or cheesecloth.

2. Add the sugar, adding more if too tart. To prepare each drink, fill a tall glass about a third full with ice. Add ½ cup plum nectar to each glass. Then add 1 shot of vodka and fill glass with seltzer, to taste, allowing a 1 inch margin at top of glass. Place a plum wedge on the edge of each glass and serve.

Herbed Sun Mint Tea

With blue skies abounding, just about everyone in the Southwest makes sun tea. After some experimenting, you'll learn the best place in your kitchen or patio to place the tea for maximum sun and for how long.

Yield: 1 gallon or enough to serve 6 generously

1 gallon cold water
¼ cup loose tea or 4 tea bags (orange pekoe or other favorite tea)
4 sprigs fresh mint
4 sprigs fresh lavender
4 sprigs fresh thyme

1. Using a glass jar, place the tea in a tea ball or hang the tea bags in the water. Wash and add the herbs. (Fresh herbs make a big difference—dried ones are not as aromatic. If you cannot get fresh ones, add about a teaspoon of each herb to the tea ball.)

2. Leave in the sun until the color deepens, 3 to 4 hours or until the tea is golden tan. Remove the tea ball or bags. The fresh herbs can stay in the tea. Serve the tea over ice with a bit of each fresh herb broken and placed in each tumbler. Do not add dried herbs.

Sage Bread Toasts with Fresh Tomato Salsa

1. Prepare the bread the day before (or several days before and freeze).

2. Slice into thin slices and toast in a moderate broiler until dry and lightly golden. Serve with a bowl of salsa to spoon over the toasts.

Sage Bread

This bread is quite moist and flavorful and wonderful just as is oozing with sweet butter. Toasting it makes for a great dipper with the Fresh Tomato Salsa. Best for toasting if made the day before.

Yield: 1 loaf

1 package dry yeast (1 scant tablespoon)
¼ cup warm water
¾ cup cottage cheese
2 eggs, beaten
1 tablespoon butter, melted
2½ cups flour
1 teaspoon salt
2 tablespoons fresh sage, minced (1 tablespoon dried)

1. Dissolve the yeast in warm water, whipping with a fork to dissolve well.

2. Place the cottage cheese in a small bowl and combine with the beaten eggs. Add the butter. Place the flour in a large bowl. Stir in the salt and the sage.

3. Combine the dissolved yeast with the cottage cheese mixture. Add all at once to the dry ingredients and stir to mix well. Place the dough on a very lightly floured board and knead it until it becomes smooth and elastic and the gluten is well developed. Cover the dough and let it rise until doubled—about an hour—and an inserted finger leaves a large hole.

4. Preheat the oven to 375°. Butter a 9-inch round pan. Punch the dough down and shape it into a round. Place it in the pan. Cover it with a cloth and allow to rise until almost doubled.

5. Bake 45 minutes or until the loaf is browned and sounds hollow when thumped. Cool 10 minutes on a rack and then remove from pan.

Fresh Tomato Salsa

Yield: 6 servings

2 large red ripe garden fresh tomatoes
2 teaspoons fresh Mexican oregano (1 teaspoon dried)
½ cup diced red onion
2 cloves fresh garlic, minced
1 teaspoon pequin quebrado chile, or to taste

Combine all ingredients and set aside until ready to serve. Allow at least 30 minutes for the flavors to marry.

Note: Pequin quebrado is the original hot crushed red chile. Supermarket substitutes on the whole are not as flavorful, but can be used.

Navajo Tacos

These have become so popular at fairs, Indian markets, and festivals that frequently the wait is 45 minutes just to get one. I prefer to remember them as a child, when often around the plazas or even under a piñon tree by the road, Navajo women would sit in their flowing skirts and fry the bread for these tacos in cast-iron pots on the end of a piñon twig. Either way, crowd or no crowd, they are wonderful!

Yield: 6 tacos

1 recipe Navajo Fry Bread (see page 73)
Beef taco filling
1¼ cups stewed beans, preferably pinto
1 medium onion, diced
1 large tomato, diced
½ head iceberg lettuce, finely sliced
1 cup coarsely grated Monterey Jack and cheddar,
  mixed
Salsa of your choice, preferably homemade*

*You can prepare your own fresh salsa easily by combining 1 cup each diced red ripe tomato, white onion and parched, peeled green chiles. Flavor with 1 minced garlic clove, 1 teaspoon salt and ½ cup coarsely chopped cilantro (optional).

1. Prepare Navajo Fry Bread dough and fry as directed. Drain well and set aside.

2. Prepare the Beef Taco Filling and the other ingredients. To assemble for serving, warm the bread disks in a 350° oven just until warm—about 5 minutes. Leave the oven on for melting the cheese.

3. Assemble each taco by scattering the ingredients on top of the Navajo Fry Bread. Top each with ⅙ of the beef, ⅙ of the beans, then the onion, lettuce, tomato, and cheese. Return tacos to the oven about 5 more minutes or until the cheese is melted. Serve with salsa as desired.

Beef Taco Filling

Yield: 6 tacos

¾ pound extra lean ground beef (no more
  than 10% fat)
1 garlic clove, minced
1 tablespoon pure ground mild chile
1 tablespoon pure ground hot chile
2 teaspoons cider vinegar

Pinch ground Mexican oregano
½ teaspoon ground cumin
½ teaspoon salt or to taste

Saute the beef and drain well. Then stir in the remaining ingredients and keep warm until ready to assemble the tacos.

Roasted Baby Blue or Red Potato Salad

Roasting the baby potatoes in the oven before preparing the salad makes the flavor so much richer. If you have access to a smoker or just happen to have smoked potatoes on hand, you can make the salad this way also.

Yield: 6 servings

3 pounds baby blue or red potatoes (available at specialty stores)
1/3 cup extra virgin Spanish olive oil
1/2 cup chopped scallions
1 teaspoon salt
1/2 cup coarsely chopped Italian flat leaf parsley
1/2 cup chopped, parched green chile, about 4 chiles (or 1 4-ounce can)
3 tablespoons white wine vinegar
Several grinds black pepper

1. Preheat the oven to 350°. Place the potatoes in a single layer on a cookie sheet. Sprinkle with 1 tablespoon of the oil, then the salt and the chopped scallions. Bake about 30 minutes or until soft when pierced with a fork.

2. When done, place the potatoes in an earthenware bowl and add the remaining oil and toss. Cover with a lid or foil for about 10 minutes to steam. Add the remaining ingredients and toss together and taste and adjust seasonings. Allow to set at room temperature for about 30 minutes before serving.

Black Mesa Apricot Crumble

In New Mexico, the apricots are special! Whether it is the high altitude and sunny climate or the soil or whatever—they are luscious, very fragrant and flavorful. Simply topped with a streusel or crumb topping, you can hardly beat it.

Yield: 6 servings

3 cups halved, seeded, unpeeled apricots (approximately 1 1/2 pounds)
1/2 cup sweet (unsalted) butter, cut in small squares
1 1/4 cups granulated sugar
2 tablespoons candied ginger, chopped
1/2 teaspoon nutmeg
1/2 cup flour
1/2 cup oatmeal

1. Preheat the oven to 375°. Butter a 9-inch square baking dish or equivalent. Place the apricots in the bottom of the baking dish.

2. Using a pastry blender or mixer, combine the rest of the ingredients until the mixture has no visible lumps. Evenly sprinkle the mixture over the top of the apricots and bake for 40 minutes or until the apricots are bubbly and the topping is lightly browned.

3. Serve as is or with ice cream, frozen yogurt, or cream.

Summer Garden's Bounty, A Vegetarian's Pleasure

M E N U

Iced Chamomile-Spearmint Sun Tea

*Grilled, Herb-Basted Summer Vegetable
Salad over Chipotle Fusilli with
Sun Dried Tomato-Balsamic Vinaigrette*

Taos Focaccia

Watermelon Sorbet with Peppered Vodka

Mexican Wedding Cakes

With the garden just bursting with bountiful vegetables, why not enjoy them in their purest state—freshly picked, grilled with fresh garden herbs and tossed into a frenzy with Chipotle Fusilli? Focaccia's warm yeasty goodness, especially when topped with mountains of onions and herbs glossed over with a crumble of sharp cheese, makes it the perfect companion to the pasta. The smoky heat of ripe, red jalapeños really sparks pasta—giving it a robust spiciness.

If you do not have your own vegetable garden, go to a farmer's market or green grocer to select very fresh vegetables that are still waxy and firm.

And who dares to think of summer without watermelon? This sorbet treats your guests to the fragrance of watermelon without all the mess. To accompany the sorbet, Mexican Wedding Cakes provide the perfect buttery crunch.

For the sunny skies overhead, bright fiesta colors are in order. Use primary colors—red, yellow, and blue placemats or table runners on a cloth that complements. If you do not have brightly colored dishes of any sort, consider the red, yellow, and blue heavy plastic plates you can purchase at party or card shops. These can even be washed in the dishwasher and tucked in your picnic basket for future use.

A table set on a terrace or patio would be best. An old picnic table or even card tables clothed in bright summery colors would be fine.

Day before (or even earlier):

Prepare the Watermelon Sorbet.
Make or buy the Mexican Wedding Cakes.
Prepare the salad dressing.

Two hours before:

Make the focaccia dough and topping.
Prepare the herb baste.
Prepare the vegetables and brush with the baste.
Portion the sorbet into goblets and freeze
 (if freezer space is available). Arrange
 the cookies on a serving plate.

Prepare the fire in the grill.
Preheat the oven to 400°, then bake the focaccia
 for 20 minutes so that it comes out of the
 oven about when the guests arrive.
Bring the salted water to a boil.

At serving time:

Serve the tea.
Grill the vegetables.
Boil the pasta to the *al dente* stage.
Prepare the vegetable pasta salad.

Iced Chamomile-Spearmint Sun Tea

This very light, yet delightful tea is very refreshing!

Yield: 1 gallon or enough to serve 6

1 gallon water
¼ cup loose chamomile tea placed in a
 tea ball or 4 tea bags
12 sprigs fresh spearmint

1. Place the water in a glass jar, then add the tea and six spearmint sprigs. Place in direct sunlight until the color deepens somewhat. With chamomile, the tea is a light golden color.

2. The tea should be ready after about two hours in the sun. Serve over ice in tall glasses garnished with a mint sprig.

Grilled, Herb-Basted Summer Vegetable Salad over Chipotle Fusilli with Sun-Dried Tomato-Balsamic Vinaigrette

Grilling vegetables adds a depth to their flavor and makes for a deeply flavored vegetable medley to toss with pasta—especially the chile-flavored ones!

Yield: 6 servings

2 small zucchini, sliced lengthwise into
  ¼-inch thick slices
2 small yellow summer squash, sliced as above
1 red onion, sliced in half-inch slices
1 red bell pepper, seeded, cored, and quartered
3 ears fresh corn, shucked, and silks removed
4 green chiles (fresh or frozen)
2 cups cooked black beans (canned are all right)

HERB BASTE

1 tablespoon fresh basil
1 tablespoon fresh rosemary
1 tablespoon fresh Mexican oregano
3 cloves garlic
3 tablespoons extra virgin olive oil

GARNISH

3 Roma tomatoes, coarsely chopped
3 scallions, dark green tops removed and thinly sliced

1. Prepare all the vegetables. Light a medium high fire on the grill or preheat the oven to 400°. Using a blender or mini-chop, blend all the herb baste ingredients together.

2. Using a pastry brush, evenly spread the herb baste on the squash, onion, bell pepper, and corn. Pierce the green chiles a couple of times each—do not spread with the baste. Grill or oven roast until the vegetables are medium—neither crisp nor soft. Remove from heat. The green chile should be somewhat charred on the outside. If oven roasting, the chiles will need to be broiled to parch them, then peeled and coarsely chopped.

3. Meanwhile, prepare the pasta and vinaigrette.

4. When the vegetables are done, slice the squash into ½ inch slices, coarsely chop the red bell pepper and onion, cut the corn from the cob, and stir together in a large bowl with the green chiles and black beans. Prepare the garnish.

5. To serve, add the cooked pasta and toss with the salad dressing. Evenly apportion onto the plates; then top with the tomato and scallion garnish. Serve with the focaccia.

Chipotle Fusilli

5 quarts water (or as the package directs)
2 teaspoons salt
1 tablespoon oil
10 ounces chipotle fusilli (spindle-shaped, short cut pasta; similar pastas, such as penne or rotini can be substituted).

Bring the water, salt, and oil to a boil in a large stewing pot, and add the pasta. Cook until *al dente*. Then drain and place in a large salad bowl.

Note: *Chipotle fusilli* is available in southwestern specialty stores and through mail order from Pecos Valley Spice Company, P.O. Box 964, Albuquerque, NM 87103; 1-800-473-TACO (8226).

Sun-Dried Tomato-Balsamic Vinaigrette

¼ cup (about 8) sun dried tomatoes
¾ cup extra virgin olive oil
⅓ cup balsamic vinegar
1 tablespoon Dijon mustard

Soak the tomatoes in the olive oil and heat briefly in a microwave or on top of the stove to soften them. Then chop finely. Whisk in the remaining ingredients and set aside.

Taos Focaccia

It is amazing that this delicious bread is as fast and easy as it is. Here we have adapted the original Italian version to feature southwestern flavors. You can make this early in the day as it is best freshly baked.

Yield: 1 large disk for 6 generous servings

3 cups all-purpose flour
1 teaspoon salt
2 teaspoons honey
1 package dry yeast (1 scant tablespoon)
1 cup warm water or more to yield a soft dough
3 tablespoons melted butter

1. Measure the flour, being careful to spoon it into the measuring cup and carefully level it off into a medium-sized bowl. Stir in the salt. In a small bowl, dissolve the yeast in warm water, add the honey, and whip with a fork. When the yeast is well dissolved, add the yeast mixture and melted butter all at once to the flour. Stir to mix well. If the dough seems quite stiff, add a bit of warm water.

2. Turn out onto a lightly floured board and knead until the dough is smooth and soft and the gluten is well developed. Cover. Prepare the topping (below).

3. Lightly butter a large baking sheet. Preheat the oven to 400°. Using a rolling pin or your fingers, spread the dough into one large disk about ¼ inch thick, allowing the outside edge to be a bit thicker to hold the topping. Poke your finger into the dough to create "pockets" 2 to 3 inches wide for the filling. Add the topping and spread all over. Top with the cheese and bake for about 20 minutes or until lightly browned. Cool on a rack for about 10 minutes and serve warm. (You can briefly reheat it.)

Focaccia Topping

¼ cup (½ stick) sweet (unsalted) butter
3 medium red onions, thinly sliced and
  separated into rounds
4 garlic cloves, minced
2 tablespoons fresh sage, minced
3 tablespoons cider vinegar
½ cup Mexican white cheese (asadero, feta,
  or goat cheese), crumbled

To prepare the topping, melt the butter, add the onions and garlic, and sauté until the onions become soft. Add all the rest of the ingredients except the cheese. Set aside.

Watermelon Sorbet with Peppered Vodka

This very refreshing dessert can be made days or a week or two ahead.

Yield: 6 servings

1 6- to 8-pound whole watermelon or section
¼ cup fresh lime juice (1 to 2 limes)
⅓ cup sugar
⅓ cup peppered vodka

1. Cut the melon off the rind, removing as many seeds as possible. Blend or process in food processor to puree, then sieve to remove the seeds.

2. Add the rest of the ingredients, tasting and adjusting flavors if desired. Place in a bowl and freeze, covered. Stir once or twice as it is freezing. To serve, scoop into footed glasses and serve with Mexican Wedding Cakes, if desired.

Mexican Wedding Cakes

These are actually cookies. If rushed for time, you could purchase these or any crisp cookie.
They can be made up to 8 months ahead of time if kept frozen.

Yield: 3 dozen

1½ cups all-purpose flour
3 tablespoons sugar
¼ teaspoon salt
¾ cup (1½ sticks) sweet (unsalted) butter
1½ teaspoons Mexican vanilla
1½ cups pecans, finely chopped
Powdered sugar

1. Pour the flour, sugar, and salt into a large mixer bowl or a food processor. Cut the butter into half-inch squares and mix together until well blended. Add the vanilla and nuts and mix until mixture holds together.

2. Preheat the oven to 325°. Butter 2 cookie sheets. Separate the dough into half-inch balls and place on cookie sheets. Bake for about 20 minutes or until firm and very lightly tan. Place the powdered sugar in a shallow bowl. While still warm, roll the cakes in the powdered sugar and allow to cool. Store in a tightly covered container.

Hot Summer
Special Dinner

✴

M E N U

Jalapeño Martinis

Posole en Escabeche
with Tostados and Hot Salsa

Chicken Avocado Fettuccine

Three Pepper Salad

Marinated Melons with Mint

Minted Iced Tea

✴

Plan this dinner when you really want to relax at your own dinner party. Most everything on the menu is easily prepared, and very little kitchen time over a hot stove is required. The only dish that needs any amount of cooking is the posole appetizer, which will have the best flavor if prepared the day before but will be delicious even made only 6 hours ahead.

The jalapeño-studded martinis will awaken the most seared late summer appetite. The fettuccine dish is spectacular and versatile—you can easily substitute seafood, such as crab or shrimp, for the chicken. The tart, tangily dressed, colorful salad, followed by the soothing, minty melon dessert, makes this a real celebration dinner.

I recommend serving this dinner in an air-conditioned dining room or on a cool porch. Complement the pastel colors of the foods with late summer flowers such as gladioli, dahlias, daisies, or asters. Use a light green or yellow cloth and napkins.

Day before (or early in the day):

Cook, cool, and marinate the posole;
    make the salsa.
Poach the chicken breast for the fettuccine.
Fry the tostadas if making them yourself.

Two hours before serving:

Prepare the melons and marinate.
Prepare the salad ingredients.
Chill the salad and dessert plates and forks.
Prepare the sauce for the fettuccine.
Brew strong dark tea, adding several sprigs of mint.
Thirty minutes before serving, place the martini
    glasses in the freezer.

At serving time:

Heat the pasta plates.
Garnish and set out the Posole en Escabeche.
    Serve with the Jalapeño Martinis.
Fifteen minutes before serving the main course,
    boil the water and cook the pasta; reheat the
    sauce.
Dress the salad and serve with the fettuccine.
Pour the iced tea and garnish each glass
    with a lemon round and a sprig of mint.
Serve the melons.

Jalapeño Martinis

For this recipe, simply prepare your favorite martini, substituting a round of pickled jalapeño for the lemon twist, olive, or pickled onion. If you don't usually make martinis, you can use either a shaker or nice glass or silver pitcher and a long-handled spoon. For 6 generous drinks, put several ice cubes in the shaker and add half a bottle of at least 80-proof gin or vodka (24 ounces, or 3 cups) and a generous optional splash or tablespoon of dry vermouth. Some omit the vermouth and add a splash of jalapeño juice from the pickled jalapeños. Be careful if you are inexperienced with this! You may want to sample the proportions ahead of time. Mix vigorously or shake to mix well. Serve garnished with a round of pickled jalapeño. (For an added touch, place the glasses in the freezer about 30 minutes before serving the drinks.)

Posole en Escabeche

Here is a very special snack or appetizer, suitable for all sorts of occasions. It is a wonderful switch from the predictable—no one who has ever tasted this mildly spicy, corn-based dish when I've served it has correctly identified its ingredients. Most people have guessed it is chicken or seafood. Do try always to use posole, *as it produces a far finer flavor than canned hominy, which should be substituted only as a last resort.*

Leftovers will keep in the refrigerator for several weeks. They can be served later as a garnish or major ingredient in a salad on a bed of lettuce, or used as a filling for an avocado half. By adding flaked crab, fish, or chicken with a topping of Creamy Salsa Verde, or a dollop of sour cream and lime, you can make a light lunch or tasty snack. Posole en Escabeche *can also be served as a garnish for egg dishes or for almost any Mexican entrée on a bed of shredded lettuce or in a lettuce leaf cup.*

Yield: 8 cups

1 package (1 pound) dry posole
¼ cup freshly squeezed lime juice
2 teaspoons salt
⅓ cup extra virgin olive oil, preferably Spanish
2 garlic cloves, minced
1½ fresh or dried bay leaves
2 leaves purple sage, chopped, or ½ teaspoon dried
¼ teaspoon Mexican oregano, ground or crushed
1 teaspoon ground cumin
1 tablespoon ground pure mild California red chile
1 large Spanish onion, thinly sliced, separated into rings
½ fresh or canned jalapeño, finely chopped
1 cup white vinegar
¼ cup chopped fresh cilantro
4 leafy lettuce leaves
6 ounces warm tostados, preferably made from blue corn (to make your own, see pages 19, 21–22)
½ cup Creamy Salsa Verde (see page 32)

1. Rinse and sort the *posole*, discarding shriveled or brown kernels. Place the good kernels in a heavy 5-quart cooking pot. Add water to cover and boil until tender—about 2 hours. As soon as the posole becomes tender but not soft, sprinkle with the lime juice and the salt. Be sure not to season until kernels have softened or they will never soften! Cool to room temperature.

2. While the *posole* is cooking, combine the oil, garlic, bay leaves, sage, oregano, cumin, ground chile, onion, jalapeño, and vinegar. Using a food processor or blender, whip until well blended, or chop the seasonings and herbs and whip with a small whisk or fork.

3. Pour over the cooled, room-temperature posole and stir well, using a gentle folding motion and taking great care to not break the *posole* kernels. Add 2 tablespoons of the cilantro and stir again. Allow to marinate, stirring occasionally, at least 4 hours or overnight. Preparing several days ahead is all right.

4. Place in a shallow Mexican or earthenware dish—rectangular, if possible—tucking leafy lettuce leaves into each corner. Garnish with the remaining 2 tablespoons of chopped cilantro.

5. To serve, the warmed tostados with Creamy Salsa Verde on the side should be accompanied by a small bowl of toothpicks.

Chicken Avocado Fettuccine

The creamy-smooth texture of Monterey Jack sauce laced with New Mexico green chiles blends luxuriously here with the subtle flavors of chicken and avocado. Do buy green noodles, as they are the best partner for the flavors of this dish.

Yield: 6 servings

5 tablespoons sweet (unsalted) butter
2 cups fresh white button mushrooms, thinly sliced in half-moons, stems attached
1½ cups cubed poached chicken breasts
Salt
Freshly ground black pepper
1½ cups half-and-half
4 ounces Monterey Jack cheese, cut into ½-inch cubes
2 green New Mexico chiles, parched, peeled, seeded, and chopped (see page 17)
12 ounces green fettuccine noodles
4 ounces thin spaghetti
2 Haas avocados, cut into 1-inch cubes
Freshly grated Parmesan and Romano cheese to taste

1. Melt 3 tablespoons of the butter in a heavy large skillet. Add the mushrooms and brown lightly. Remove to a plate.

2. Melt the remaining 2 tablespoons butter in the skillet and add the cubed chicken. Brown lightly. Season with salt and freshly ground pepper.

3. Return the mushrooms to the skillet and add 1 cup of the half-and-half, the cubed cheese, and the green chiles. Cook only until the sauce thickens, 3 to 5 minutes, over medium-low heat. Remove from heat. Cover and set aside.

4. About 15 minutes before serving, bring 5 to 6 cups of water and 1 tablespoon salt to a boil in a large pot. When it boils, add the noodles, then the spaghetti, and cook about 9 minutes, or until al dente. Meanwhile, peel the avocados by first scoring with a sharp knife, then removing the peel.

5. Reheat the sauce, taking care not to let it bubble up. Add remaining ½ cup half-and-half. Cube the avocado. When the pasta is done, drain, rinse with hot water, and return to the pot. Add the sauce and toss. Serve on warm plates with a side dish of freshly grated Parmesan and Romano. Garnish each serving with avocado cubes.

Note: To poach chicken, either whole or in parts: place chicken in a deep, heavy pot (place whole chicken with breast side up). The top of the chicken should be at least three inches below the rim. Add double rich chicken broth to cover breast. Bring to a simmer and reduce heat to low simmer, cover with a close-fitting lid, and poach until joints wiggle easily. Remove from heat, cool in the broth, debone, and remove skin. (To make double rich broth, simmer chicken stock until it is reduced by half.)

Three Pepper Salad

A beautiful vision of summer! Any time you can get large, waxy, blemish-free red, yellow, and green bell peppers, try this colorful salad, which is especially pretty served on a bed of fluffy, purple-edged leaf lettuce.

Yield: 6 servings

2 garlic cloves, minced
½ cup extra virgin olive oil, preferably Spanish
1 each large green, red, and yellow bell peppers
1 large head red leaf lettuce
¼ cup red wine vinegar

1. At least 1 hour before serving, marinate the garlic in the oil. Then cut the peppers into long thin strips, removing all the ribs and seeds. Rinse, drain, and chill the lettuce.

2. Chill the salad bowls—clear glass ones are best if you have them. Chill the salad forks. Combine the vinegar with the garlic oil and shake.

3. To serve, place the lettuce leaves in the bowls. Add the peppers and lace with the vinaigrette. Serve with a pepper grinder.

Marinated Melons with Mint

To provide a cool, soothing, and perfectly simple ending to a southwestern meal I always like to marry the perfume flavor of a ripe, deep green honeydew with the less predictable Persian or Casaba melon and tingle the edges with fresh lime, mint, and a drizzle of honey.

Yield: 6 servings

½ large ripe honeydew melon
½ to ⅓ Persian or Casaba melon
Juice of 2 limes
½ cup fresh spearmint or peppermint leaves, coarsely chopped and crushed, reserving 6 perfect three-leaf sprigs
¼ cup fragrant blossom honey

1. Cut the honeydew lengthwise into six portions. Then carefully cut away from the rind and score into bite-size portions, not cutting completely through the flesh. Place on serving plates, preferably clear glass or pastel plates.

2. Cube the Persian melon. Randomly place on the honeydew. Combine the lime juice, ½ cup mint leaves, and honey—warming if thick.

3. Two hours before serving, drizzle the juice mixture over the melon and set aside loosely covered at room temperature. To serve, garnish with the mint sprigs.

Festive Formal Dinner for Four

❦

M   E   N   U

Perfect Margaritas

Marinated Mexican Mushrooms

*Creamy Chilled Cucumber Sopa
with Cheesed Tortilla Strips*

Melon Sorbet

*Swordfish with Anchovy-Caper Butter
Grilled over Mesquite*

Pasta Shells with Caribe and Eggplant

Watercress-Jicama Salad

*Double Blueberry Delight
with Crème Fraîche*

Coffee

❦

Consider this menu when you're in the mood for a somewhat extravagant dinner party that is not too difficult to manage. This dinner is a showcase for the foods of late summer, and from the Perfect Margaritas down to the Double Blueberry Delight, you'll be very pleased with how smoothly the flavors flow.

Some early preparation makes it possible to add the finishing touches with minimal kitchen time. The dinner should be served in seven courses, starting with the Marinated Mexican Mushrooms and the margaritas offered in the living room or on the patio. Then serve each item formally, using your finest china, crystal, and sterling on a snowy white linen tablecloth. White roses make a lovely centerpiece.

MENU PLAN

Day before (or early in the day):

Prepare the Marinated Mexican Mushrooms.

Prepare the Creamy Chilled Cucumber Sopa and Cheesed Tortilla Strips.

Prepare the Melon Sorbet.

Two hours before:

Prepare the Anchovy-Caper Butter.

Prepare the sauce for the pasta dish.

Slice the eggplant, salt it, and place between layers of paper toweling; 30 minutes later, dice and fry the eggplant. Set out the kettle with water for boiling the pasta and all remaining ingredients.

Prepare the jícama, rinse the watercress, and make the salad dressing. Chill separately.

Prepare the Double Blueberry Delight with Créme Fraîche.

Frost the glasses for the margaritas. Chill the wine, salad plates, soup bowls, and goblets or sherbets for dessert.

Set out the coffeemaker.

Start the fire to grill the fish.

At serving time:

Add the 1 cup fresh berries to the cooked blueberries.

Make the margaritas just before the guests are expected to arrive.

Set out the Marinated Mexican Mushrooms and serve with the margaritas.

About 15 minutes before serving the soup, warm the Cheesed Tortilla Strips and boil the water for the pasta. Heat the plates for the fish and the pasta.

Boil the pasta while you serve the cucumber soup with the tortilla strips.

Start to grill the fish.

Warm the sauce and eggplant for the pasta dish.

Turn the fish and serve the sorbet.

Serve the fish on heated plates.

Combine the ingredients for the pasta dish and serve on heated plates.

Toss the jícama and watercress with the dressing and serve the salad on chilled plates.

Perfect Margaritas

Be prepared! These high-octane margaritas just might sweep some of your guests off their feet. They are wonderfully flavored and potent. For the very best margaritas always squeeze fresh limes, preferably the juicy, thin-skinned, yellowish Mexican variety, which have the traditional pungent flavor. Whenever I am near the Mexican border or in the Caribbean, I lay aside quantities of the freshly squeezed juice of these limes in half-pint freezer containers or jars and bring them home solidly frozen. In a pinch the dark green, thicker-skinned Persian limes will work, too. Be sure to keep the juice frozen until you use it.

Always buy at least 80 proof tequila, made from the blue agave plant, sometimes called mezcal in Spanish or mescal in English. The very finest tequilas are 92 proof. To be labeled all natural, with the NOM seal, the Mexican tequila distillers association requires that only 100 percent blue agave be used. Under Mexican law, however, tequila need contain only as little as 51 percent blue agave in order to be called tequila. These products contain sugar, water, or caramel coloring extenders.

Offer only one round—at most two—before serving the delectable dinner. The Marinated Mexican Mushrooms are a delicious cocktail nibble alongside the margaritas.

Yield: 4 large margaritas

8 fresh limes, preferably Mexican variety
Coarse salt
¹/₂ cup triple sec, or to taste
1¹/₂ cups 80- to 92-proof pure agave tequila (usually the white is preferred, however you can use the gold if you have a personal preference)
¹/₃ of a fresh egg white, beaten with a fork
Crushed ice

1. Squeeze the limes, being certain to get all the flesh plus the juice. Measure and use only ½ cup juice. Reserve the rest.

2. Prepare the glasses. If salt is desired, rub one of the lime rinds around the top rim of each glass. Crunch the glasses into the salt and place in the freezer—allowing at least 30 minutes to frost.

3. Meanwhile, prepare the margaritas by placing the lime juice, triple sec, tequila, and egg white in the blender. Add enough ice to fill the blender about halfway. Process. If the texture is not slushy enough, add ice to get the desired texture. Taste and add more triple sec if not sweet enough. Serve immediately in the frosted glasses, either straight up or over ice.

Note: You can freeze leftover margaritas for at least a month.

Marinated Mexican Mushrooms

Since I first sampled them in Hermosillo, Mexico, these mushrooms have been a favorite of mine. None ever goes begging, but should any be left, they are delicious as a salad dressing.

Yield: 4 servings

12 ounces 2- to 3-inch white button mushrooms,
*   wiped clean and stemmed*
⅓ cup virgin olive oil
⅓ cup white wine vinegar
2 garlic cloves, minced
1 teaspoon caribe (crushed dried red chile)
½ teaspoon Mexican oregano
¼ teaspoon salt
1 large Spanish onion, thinly sliced and separated
*   into rings*
Caribe chile for garnish

1. Put the prepared mushrooms in a heatproof bowl. Bring the next six ingredients to a boil, adding the onions once the mixture begins to boil. Cook and stir frequently until the onions just begin to lose their crispness.

2. Pour the mixture over the mushrooms, and let them marinate at room temperature for at least 2 hours, stirring frequently.

3. Chill about ½ hour—not longer—or the oil will thicken. The mushrooms can be made several days before —they keep very well up to a week. They are attractive served in a shallow rectangular or oval bowl, with the mushrooms arranged around the edges and the onions in the center. Add a sprinkle of the caribe for a special touch. Serve with toothpicks.

Creamy Chilled Cucumber Sopa

This quickly prepared sopa, or soup, is also good for a light lunch with finger sandwiches or a salad. It will keep up to three days in the refrigerator.

Yield: 4 servings

1 tablespoon sweet (unsalted) butter

1 medium cucumber, peeled, seeded, and coarsely chopped

4 tablespoons sliced green onions (scallions), very thinly cut, greens and all (discard the coarse ends)

1¼ cups skim milk

1 teaspoon (1 packet) chicken bouillon granules

2 tablespoons coarsely chopped cilantro

½ cup plain no-fat yogurt

1 tablespoon pure ground mild red chile

1. In a small saucepan, melt the butter, then add the cucumber and 2 tablespoons of the onion and cook and stir until the cucumber becomes clear and somewhat soft, about 3 minutes.

2. Put in a blender or food processor, add the milk, chicken bouillon, and 1 tablespoon of the cilantro. Process until smooth. Stir in the yogurt. Pour into a small pitcher or bowl and chill.

3. To serve, pour into small bowls, cups, or wine glasses and garnish with the remaining cilantro. Sprinkle with the mild chile.

Cheesed Tortilla Strips

A great topper for soups and salads, Cheesed Tortilla Strips might be considered a kind of Tex-Mex crouton. They are also a great way to use tired corn tortillas. For a variation, you can leave them plain, or sprinkle with chile or other spices.

Yield: 4 servings

2 corn tortillas, cut into strips ½ inch wide and 3 inches long (discard the odd-shaped corner pieces or reserve for later use to thicken a soup or stew, or use in meatloaf)

1 quart cooking oil

½ cup grated Monterey Jack cheese

1. Cut the tortilla strips while the oil is heating to 375°. Fry, a batch at a time, in a fry basket until the bubbles subside and the strips are crisp and golden.

2. Quickly drain each batch on paper toweling, place on a cookie sheet, and sprinkle with the cheese while still hot. When all are fried, place in a 350° oven for 10 to 15 minutes to melt the cheese. They should be warmed if prepared in advance.

Variation: For a low-fat version, bake the strips until crisp and golden on a cookie sheet in a 400° oven for about eight minutes. Sprinkle with cheese and melt.

Melon Sorbet

Melons—expecially watermelon—have been a special favorite of the Pueblo Indians in New Mexico for centuries. The mountain range sheltering the east side of Albuquerque is named Sandia, *a Spanish word, also used by the Pueblo Indians, that means watermelon—a fruit they stash away in caves between layers of straw. I have been served watermelon in pueblo homes even in winter. Although its flesh had almost caramelized into a deep, rosy-tan color, it was wonderfully flavored.*

This simple summery palate-cleanser is refreshing as either a course after spicy foods or as a dessert. Choose an extra ripe, thumping good watermelon for the best flavor. Sorbet is a wonderful way to preserve summer's bounty, as it will keep its flavor for about six months in the freezer.

Yield: 2 quarts

8 cups cubed, seeded watermelon, honeydew, or cantaloupe
Juice of 1 fresh lime, preferably Mexican variety (at least 3 teaspoons)

1. Process the melon and lime juice in a blender or food processor until it is frothy and pulpy. Place in a large bowl, preferably stainless steel as it will freeze best.

2. Place on the bottom of the freezer and stir every 30 minutes until firm. This takes about 3 hours. If making the sorbet in advance, place it in the refrigerator 2 to 3 hours before serving. To serve, make little balls of sorbet, using a round teaspoon or melon scoop, and place 3 to 5 in a fluted wine glass.

Swordfish with Anchovy-Caper Butter Grilled Over Mesquite

Elegant and easy, this grilled dish is distinguished by the special smokiness of mesquite, a flavor many have come to love. If mesquite is hard to find, substitute a good hardwood charcoal, tossing on some wood chips of hickory, oak, or fruitwood, or use grapevine cuttings.

Shark or other firm-fleshed, substantial fish can be substituted for the swordfish. The lime in the butter is a delightful, light, and delicious foil for the strength of the anchovies.

Yield: 4 servings

1 large lime
¼ pound sweet (unsalted) butter, at room temperature
1 tin (2 ounces) flat anchovy fillets
2 tablespoons capers (in vinegar or salt)
4 swordfish steaks, 6 to 8 ounces each
1 small bunch watercress, rinsed

1. Build a small fire of mesquite or other hardwood charcoal briquets and let it rest and become white coals. If using charcoal, toss on some soaked wood chips. When it smolders a good bit, you are ready to grill the fish.

2. Meanwhile, squeeze the lime and mix it into the butter, adding smashed anchovies and the capers. Mix in a mortar or in a small heavy bowl.

3. Oil the grill with a cloth soaked with vegetable oil. Hold the cloth with tongs to coat the grill well and prevent burning your fingers. Raise the rack to a height of 6 inches above the coals.

4. Place the fish on the grill and sear the first side. After about 5 minutes, turn and grill the other side. Five minutes later, check to be sure the flesh is cooked. It should be very moist and dull looking, not shiny like raw fish.

5. When the fish is done, arrange it on warmed plates and place a large spoonful of the Anchovy-Caper Butter on each serving. Garnish each plate with a handful of watercress.

Pasta Shells with Caribe and Eggplant

The hearty flavor of this pasta preparation is a perfect accompaniment to any subtle seafood, veal, or chicken dish.

Yield: 4 servings

2 tablespoons plus ¼ cup virgin olive oil,
    preferably Spanish
1 can (1 pound) crushed Italian plum tomatoes
1 tablespoon minced fresh basil leaves,
    or 1 teaspoon dried
1½ teaspoons finely chopped fresh oregano,
    or ½ teaspoon dried
1 eggplant, about 1 pound
1½ teaspoons salt
8 ounces pasta shells
1 tablespoon salad oil
¼ cup freshly grated Romano cheese
1½ teaspoons caribe (crushed dried red chile)

1. Heat 2 tablespoons olive oil, then add the tomatoes, basil, and oregano. Allow to simmer over very low heat.

2. Meanwhile, cut the rinsed eggplant into ½-inch-thick slices. Generously salt each side of the slices, using the 1½ teaspoons salt. Place between double sheets of paper toweling. Top with another layer, always making sure to place the toweling between layers. Allow the eggplant to set for about 30 minutes. Press toweling against eggplant to remove moisture and salt.

3. Cut the eggplant into ½-inch cubes. Heat the ¼ cup olive oil in a very large heavy skillet. Add the cubes of eggplant and cook and turn until each square is browned. Set aside.

4. About 15 minutes before serving, bring 4 quarts of salted water to a boil, adding 1 tablespoon salad oil.

5. Add the pasta and cook according to the package instructions—6 to 8 minutes—or until it is *al dente*. Taste the sauce and adjust the seasoning.

6. To serve, place the drained pasta shells in a large heated bowl. Add the sauce and the fried eggplant cubes. Sprinkle with the cheese and the caribe and toss well. Taste and adjust flavors, if desired.

Watercress-Jícama Salad

Light, delicate-looking, and tangily dressed, Watercress-Jícama Salad sets the scene ideally for the dessert to follow.

Yield: 4 servings

1 cup peeled jícama cut in long, slender matchsticks
1 fresh lime
1 teaspoon crushed ristra or caribe chile, or
  other crushed dried red chile
1 teaspoon coarse sea salt
1/2 cup walnut oil
1/4 cup raspberry vinegar
1 large garlic clove, crushed
1 teaspoon Dijon mustard
1 good-sized bunch of watercress, rinsed,
  with stems removed

1. Cover a shallow pan with wax paper and lay the jícama out in a single layer. Squeeze lime juice over it, then sprinkle with the chile and salt. Allow to marinate for 30 minutes.

2. Meanwhile, prepare the salad dressing, combining the oil, vinegar, garlic, and mustard; whisk and set aside.

3. Chill the jícama and watercress until serving time. Combine at the very last moment, lightly tossing with the dressing.

Double Blueberry Delight with Crème Fraîche

I discovered this dessert quite by accident one weekend while cooking at our Woodstock cottage, which has bountiful blueberries growing up the mountainside, both wild and domestic. With such abundance, I've had great fun experimenting, and am quite pleased with the friendly flavors of this dish, especially when it follows a meal with a complex array of tastes. You can substitute almost any berry here and even prepare the dish a day or two ahead.

Yield: 4 servings

1 pint ripe blueberries
1/2 cup freshly squeezed orange juice
1/2 cup sugar, or more to taste
1 teaspoon freshly grated orange zest
1 teaspoon freshly grated lemon zest
A few grinds of fresh nutmeg (a generous pinch)
1 ounce Grand Marnier or Cointreau
1/2 cup (4 ounces) crème fraîche
8 to 12 finely cut fresh orange rind curls

1. Rinse and sort the blueberries, discarding any that are not good. Reserve 1 cup of fresh berries. Place the balance in a small heavy saucepan.

2. Add the orange juice, sugar, and zests. Cook over low heat until the berries cook down, about 30 minutes. Then add the nutmeg and liqueur. Taste and adjust the seasoning if desired—the flavor should be somewhat intense. Cool in a medium-size earthenware or stoneware bowl. Before serving the appetizers, add the uncooked blueberries.

3. To serve, place in goblets and top each with a tablespoon of crème fraîche and a few fresh curls of finely sliced zested orange rind.

IV ❦ Fall

Balloon Launch Brunch

M E N U

Sunrise Sippers

New Mexican Crab-Cannellini Bruschettas

*Blue Horizon Blue Breakfast Burritos
with Blue Corn Crepes
and Bleu Cheese-Chile Sauce*

*Baby Greens Salad with
Honey-Mustard Vinaigrette*

Pear Breakfast Cake

Coffee

The International Balloon Fiesta is Albuquerque's most spectacular fall event. Due to the special setting of the city, the balloon flight pattern is a box of sizable proportions—enough to accommodate gracefully over one thousand balloons that are brought from all over the world to fly in special events.

To make the most of the occasion, it is best to go to the Balloon Park very early—before sunrise. Since this event is always conducted in early October, the mornings are chilly and brisk, making the Sunrise Sippers quite a welcome treat. This menu is great for any tailgate or camp-out brunch.

While everyone is sipping away, serve the New Mexican Crab-Cannellini Bruschettas. Then you can take your time getting the rest of the menu ready for serving. I'd recommend serving tailgate style if in a crowded setting. If serving picnic style on the ground, bring a warm, colorful blanket for a serving and seating background.

The type of table covering or cloth will be dictated by the space where you plan to serve. Blankets or quilts are quite appropriate for this type of menu.

Use practical dishes and glasses. Bright plastic or tinware is perfect because breakage is not a problem and packing is much easier. Or you may wish to select attractive paper plates, glasses, or cups.

MENU PLAN

Day before (or several days before):

If desired, the Pear Cake can be made and frozen several days ahead. Or bake just the day before.

Prepare the crepes and separate each with waxed paper.

Prepare the crab and toast the bread.

Prepare the Bleu Cheese-Chile Sauce and place in a heat-proof container.

Rinse the salad greens, spin, place in a covered container, and chill.

Prepare the honey dressing and place in a transportable jar with a tight-fitting lid.

One hour before:

Heat the oven to 200° and place the pear cake in it, as well as the container of bleu cheese sauce and the crepes.

Make the coffee.

Scramble the eggs and roll in the crepes. Wrap in foil and place in the oven on a tray until departure.

When ready to go, wrap heavy newspaper around all the warm foods and place in a box or carrying container. Place the food in a thermal insulated picnic hamper, if you have one.

At serving time:

Mix and serve the Sunrise Sippers; serve the New Mexican Crab-Cannellini Bruschettas.

Prepare the serving area, on the tailgate, table, or blanket.

Serve the burritos with the sauce.

Toss the salad with the dressing and serve with the burritos.

Cut and serve the Pear Breakfast Cake.

Sunrise Sippers

Just before sunup, these not only taste great, but the medley of liquors supplies just the right "kick" to give the day a bright beginning. Carry the coffee in a thermos and the liquors in their own bottles or you can premix the liquors.

Yield: 6 drinks

6 cups of good quality French roast type coffee
3 tablespoons Grand Marnier
3 tablespoons Kahlúa
3 tablespoons amaretto
3 tablespoons brandy or cognac
Whipped cream in aerosol can
Freshly ground cinnamon

Place the coffee in 6 mugs, then top each with 1½ teaspoons each of the 4 liqueurs (or combine them and then measure 2 tablespoons of the liqueur mixture on top of each mug. Add the whipped cream and serve with a dash of cinnamon on top if desired.

New Mexican Crab-Cannellini Bruschettas

The flavorful crab and bean salsa is absolutely delicious and will keep a few days in the refrigerator—perfect as an appetizer any time of day! Served on crisp toasts of Italian or French bread, it's a hearty snack.

Yield: 6 servings

6 red radishes, rinsed and thinly sliced
8 to 10 small green onions, thinly sliced
1½ cup red bell pepper, diced
½ cup green bell pepper, diced
½ cup jícama, peeled and diced
¼ cup coarsely chopped Italian parsley
1 16-ounce can white or cannellini beans, drained
*1 tablespoon caribe, crushed northern
    New Mexico chile*
2 limes, juiced
*½ pound crab flakes, any kind—even Serimi
    artificial crab is good*
*1 medium-sized loaf (about a pound) Italian
    or French bread, unsliced*

1. Using a medium-sized mixing bowl, combine all the ingredients except the bread. Taste and adjust seasonings. Make at least the night before serving.

2. Preheat the oven to 450°. Slice the bread into ¾-inch slices and place in a single layer on a cookie sheet. Toast the bread about 5 minutes to a golden brown, watching carefully, and remove to a cooling rack. (This can be done a day or so ahead.)

3. To serve, place the toasts on a tray or platter and serve with the salsa. Do not "plate up" ahead of time, as the toast will get soggy.

Blue Horizon Blue Breakfast Burritos
with Blue Corn Crepes and Bleu Cheese-Chile Sauce

The double combination of the blue corn crepes surrounding a green chile-egg scramble with bleu cheese sauce makes these truly unique and delicious! They are just perfect for watching a balloon launch or for any tailgate type party. They are wonderful served right from your dining room, kitchen, or patio. Depending on the hour you are serving this brunch, you can make the crepes ahead of time and have the eggs ready to scramble.

Yield: 6 servings

1 recipe Blue Corn Crepes (see recipe next page)
12 eggs
½ cup milk—can be skim
6 fresh green chiles or about ⅔ cup, chopped
1 teaspoon ground Mexican oregano
¾ teaspoon salt
2 teaspoons butter
1 recipe Bleu Cheese-Chile Sauce (see recipe next page)

1. Prepare the crepes, using the recipe below. Just before serving, whisk the eggs with ½ cup milk. Add the green chiles, Mexican oregano, and salt.

2. Meanwhile, heat a large heavy skillet with the butter using medium heat. Add the eggs mixture, stirring constantly, and turn down the heat to low. Cook and stir until the eggs are of desired doneness, and still medium soft.

3. Allowing two burritos per person, lay out 12 warm crepes flat. (If the crepes were made ahead, warm slightly in the microwave in a plastic bag for about 1 minute, or heat in foil in a moderate oven.) Place the eggs in a strip down the center of each crepe, leaving a 1- to 1½-inch margin at the bottom of each. To roll, first fold the crepe up from the bottom and then fold in the two sides and press together. They should hold together—if not, secure briefly with a toothpick pierced in vertically. To transport the burritos, wrap each in heavy foil, sealing well.

4. Serve napped (or ribboned) with the Bleu Cheese-Chile Sauce.

Blue Corn Crepes

These light, delicate crepes are wonderful for burritos and other fillings.
The batter works best if allowed to rest for at least an hour before baking.

Yield: 12 crepes

¾ *cup flour*
¼ *cup blue corn flour or meal*
¼ *teaspoon salt*
⅛ *teaspoon cumin*
¾ *cup water*
⅔ *cup milk*
3 *eggs, beaten with a whisk*
2 *tablespoons melted sweet (unsalted) butter*
1 *tablespoon vegetable oil*

1. Measure the dry ingredients, taking care to spoon the flour gently into the measuring cup before leveling. Place in a medium-sized bowl. Combine the liquid ingredients and stir into the flours until mixed. Do not beat. Add the butter and set aside.

2. Heat a 6- to 8-inch heavy skillet over medium heat. Brush with the oil. A drop of batter should sizzle when hot enough. Using a ¼-cup measure or 4-ounce ladle, place a scant ladleful of batter in the hot skillet and tip to coat the bottom of the skillet evenly. When the surface bubbles and looks dry, turn and cook the other side. Remove when done and repeat, adding oil to skillet only when needed.

3. Keep the crepes warm by placing in a cloth or crock until serving

Bleu Cheese-Chile Sauce

This simple bechamel or white sauce can be used with numerous dishes—over souffles,
poached eggs, burritos, and so on. Just omit the bleu cheese and flavor as desired.

3 *tablespoons sweet (unsalted) butter*
3 *tablespoons flour*
2½ *cups chicken stock*
⅓ *to* ½ *cup bleu cheese or to taste*
A few drops liquid hot pepper sauce such as Tabasco

1. In a heavy saucepan, melt the butter over medium heat. When slightly browned, stir in the flour. Stirring constantly, allow the roux to tan lightly. Add a bit of chicken stock, stirring continuously.

2. Continue to add more stock, stirring constantly until all the stock is added. Season with the cheese and allow to melt. Taste and add more cheese if desired. Add the hot pepper sauce. Serve warm. To transport to the park, place in a thermal bowl or wide-mouthed thermos.

Baby Greens Salad with Honey-Mustard Vinaigrette

Use any combination of lettuces and edible blossoms for this salad.

1½ quarts mixed baby lettuces or mesclun mix
12 to 18 pansy or nasturtium blossoms
1 recipe Honey-Mustard Vinaigrette, recipe below

1. Rinse the greens and spin or blot dry. Place in a chilled salad bowl.

2. To serve, grind a few grates of fresh pepper over the top, then add the dressing and lightly toss. Serve on chilled plates if possible.

Honey-Mustard Vinaigrette

This delightfully tart dressing is wonderful on any assortment of greens or fruit.

Yield: 6 servings

⅓ cup extra virgin Spanish olive oil
3 tablespoons freshly squeezed lemon juice
1 tablespoon aromatic honey, such as sage or mesquite
1 tablespoon Dijon style mustard

In a liquid measuring cup, combine all the ingredients and whisk. Chill and reserve until ready to serve over chilled greens.

Pear Breakfast Cake

Pears always seem like fall. However, I like them any time of year. Their mellow, earthy sweet taste is wonderful in salads, a wide range of desserts, and just simply fresh, eaten out of the hand. This cake is best if allowed to set after baking and served either warm or at room temperature.

Yield: 6 servings

1½ cups plus 2 tablespoons all-purpose flour
½ cup granulated sugar, divided (2 tablespoons for batter, ⅓ cup for topping, 2 teaspoons to sprinkle over the top)
¾ teaspoon salt
1½ teaspoons baking powder
1½ teaspoons ground cinnamon
¼ cup (½ stick) sweet (unsalted) butter, cut into ½ inch squares
½ cup milk
3 eggs
2 teaspoons vanilla, Mexican if possible
¾ cup sour cream
3 firm, ripe pears
A sprinkle of ground cinnamon
Confectioners' sugar
Paper doily

1. Preheat the oven to 375°, making sure the rack is in the upper third of the oven. Butter a 9 x 9-inch square cake pan. Combine the dry ingredients, reserving 2 tablespoons of flour and ⅓ cup, 2 teaspoons of the granulated sugar in a separate bowl. Stir in the salt, baking powder, and cinnamon.

2. Using your hands, a pastry blender, or the beater blade of the mixer, cut in the butter. Mix until uniform and no large particles of butter remain. In a separate small bowl, combine the milk, eggs, and vanilla and stir into the above dry ingredients. Spread the batter evenly into the buttered pan.

3. Combine the reserved 2 tablespoons of flour, ⅓ cup granulated sugar, and sour cream and pour this over the batter.

4. Peel, quarter, and core the pears. Then cut into long medium thick slices and arrange overlapping in a large circle just inside the edge of the pan. Place the remaining pears in a circle inside that one. Cover with foil and bake for 20 minutes.

5. Remove the foil and sprinkle with the remaining 2 teaspoons sugar and cinnamon. Bake for another 30 minutes or until an inserted knife comes out clean and the pears are tender and lightly browned.

6. To serve, place a paper doily on the cake and sieve some powdered sugar over it using the holes in the doily to make a pattern. Remove the doily and place foil over the top if you are transporting the cake. Otherwise serve it warm right from the oven or a serving tray.

Fall Brunch

M E N U

Southwestern Brandy Alexanders

Mango and Jambon Quesadillas
Yucatán Style

Breaded Breakfast Bacon

Jan's Cazuela

Ginger-Lemon Crumb Cake

Coffee

Fall's bountiful harvest is reason enough for bringing together friends or relatives to celebrate. However, this menu can be enjoyed anytime —whether there is a celebration at hand or not. When I first planned it, I thought of a forthcoming wedding, anniversary, graduation, birth or other life event. But no need to wait for that.

All of these dishes are very special and truly wonderful together, from the old-fashioned velvety flavor of the Alexanders to the richness of the truly decadent breaded bacon preceded by the excitement of the mango and ham *quesadillas* that really set the scene. The *cazuela* with its hearty flavor is topped off with the tart and spicy Ginger-Lemon Crumb Cake. What could be more fun?

A quilt or autumn-colored cloth, or placemats, maybe homemade with handwork or crocheted edgings, would be pretty. Fall leaves, chrysanthemums, and baby pumpkin, or gourds would be most appropriate for a centerpiece, and they could also be arranged discreetly around the room.

The setting should be the dining room, if possible. On a beautiful day, the porch or patio would also be fine.

Day before (or several days before):

Prepare the tomatillo salsa if making it.
Dice the ham and grate the cheeses for the
 quesadillas and the *cazuela*.
Prepare the fresh bread crumbs for the bacon.
Prepare the peppers and chiles for the cazuela.
A day or so ahead, bake the cake.

Two hours before:

Bread the bacon and begin baking it one hour
 ahead. When done, reduce the oven to 200°.
Prepare the *quesadillas* and keep warm in a
 200° oven.
Warm the dinner plates in 200° oven.
Set out the coffeemaker.

Thirty minutes before serving, saute and drain
 the *chorizo* for the *cazuela* and then begin the
 cazuela, browning the potatoes and onion,
 ready for finishing.

At serving time:

Prepare and serve the Southwestern
 Brandy Alexanders.
Place the crumb cake in the warm oven when
 removing the *quesadillas* and their plates.
 Cut, garnish and serve the *quesadillas*.
Fifteen minutes before serving the *cazuela*,
 finish preparing it and serve.
Serve the crumb cake and coffee.

Southwestern Brandy Alexanders

The wedding shower brunch for one of my cousins at the Shawnee Country Club in Topeka, Kansas, was my first introduction to these delicious breakfast or after dinner drinks. Beware, they are stronger than you might think! What makes these southwestern is that I've substituted Kahlúa for the dark crème de cacao. You can make them either way, using the same measurements.

Yield: 6 drinks

1 cup brandy
¾ cup Kahlua
¾ cup heavy cream
8 to 12 ice cubes

Using a blender, place all the ingredients in the jar and process until well mixed. Strain out any remaining ice cubes and serve in wide-footed drink glasses or wine glasses.

Mango and Jambon Quesadillas, Yucatán Style

These are wonderful! You can make them ahead and keep them warm in the oven while warming the plates.

Yield: 6 servings

2 tablespoons melted sweet (unsalted) butter
6 medium (6- to 8-inch) flour tortillas
1½ cups grated asadero cheese, Monterey Jack,
*   or combination of Jack and cheddar*
3 thin slices fully cooked ham, diced
1 large or 2 small ripe mangoes, peeled and diced
1 cup Cold Salsa Verde (see page 32), optional
½ cup sour cream
Lettuce or watercress to garnish

1. Preheat the oven to 250°. Preheat a griddle or *comal* on medium high heat. Using a pastry brush, lightly brush the preheated griddle or *comal* with the butter, forming it in a half-circle the size of half the tortilla.

2. Place the tortilla up with the buttered half-circle and place it on the griddle. Add ¼ cup grated cheese, spreading it in a half-circle allowing a 1-inch margin around the edge.

3. Add ⅙ of the ham and mango, reserving a few pieces of the mango for a garnish. Then fold the top of the tortilla over the filling. Grill until the first half is lightly browned and the cheese is beginning to melt. (You can tell this by gently pulling the tortilla apart to peek at the cheese.) Brush the top side of the tortilla with a bit of melted butter and turn to brown the second side. Place on a cookie sheet in a warm 250° oven. Warm the plates.

4. Continue until all 6 have been made. To serve, place each on a cutting board and cut as a pie into wedges. Then place on the warm plate and spoon the tomatillo salsa over the center of the points where they come together. Top with a dollop of sour cream, the reserved mango bits, the lettuce garnish, and serve.

❈ ❈ ❈

Breaded Breakfast Bacon

This somewhat decadent way to prepare bacon is fabulous! Baking the bacon in a comfy, flavorful crumb coating—you do drain the fat—is outrageous, making it maybe not so insulting to the waistline. Do make fresh bread crumbs—they are a must!

Yield: 6 servings

*1 cup fresh bread crumbs, made from 6 to
    8 pieces of day-old crusty white bread*
2 beaten egg whites
1 teaspoon prepared mustard such as Dijon
2 tablespoons Worcestershire sauce
12 thick country style slices of bacon

1. Preheat the oven to 325°—you can bake the bacon ahead of time and keep it warm with the quesadillas. Place the bread crumbs on a plate.

2. In a long, shallow bowl, combine the egg whites, mustard, and Worcestershire sauce, beating with a whisk or fork. Coat each piece of bacon on both sides with the egg mixture. Then dip into the crumbs. Place each piece in a single layer on a shallow baking pan or rimmed cookie sheet. Bake until crisp—about 20 minutes. Drain the fat and keep warm until serving time.

Jan's Cazuela

A cazuela *is a Mexican stove-top casserole pan and the name is used for the combination dish. This recipe can be prepared and served in the same dish—so use an oval copper casserole or any similar cooking-serving pan that can go on top of the range.*

Yield: 6 servings

1 tablespoon sweet (unsalted) butter
6 cups shredded raw potatoes, about 4 large or 6 medium
½ cup chopped onion
1 red bell pepper, roasted, peeled, and diced
3 green chiles, roasted, peeled, and diced or 1 4-ounce can
4 chorizo links, sautéed lightly, crumbled, and drained
9 eggs
1 teaspoon salt
½ teaspoon Mexican oregano
¾ cup coarsely shredded Monterey Jack and cheddar cheeses
Minced chives
1 tomato, sliced in 12 wedges

1. Melt the butter in the casserole serving dish. Add the potatoes and cook until they brown on the first side; then turn and lightly brown the second side. Add the onion and cook until clear.

2. You can cook the *cazuela* up to this point and have the rest of the ingredients ready for just combining and cooking for about 15 minutes or until the eggs just set. To prepare for serving, heat the potato-onion mixture on medium heat until warm; add the peppers and chiles and stir. Then stir in the chorizo. Beat the eggs with a whisk, and season with the salt and Mexican oregano. Pour over the potatoes and onions and cover. If no close-fitting lid is available, cover with heavy foil.

3. Cook covered for about 5 minutes, then peek. When the eggs are almost set, sprinkle with the cheese. Cook until the eggs are just set.

4. Slice the *cazuela* into 6 wedges, being careful not to score your casserole pan. Serve individually or let guests serve themselves. Garnish each wedge with a sprinkle of chives and a couple of wedges of tomato.

Ginger-Lemon Crumb Cake

The spiciness of ginger paired with the tartness of lemon brings to mind the crisp air of fall. The first time I made this we all had seconds, even though our dinner had been quite filling. I'm sure you will enjoy this too. Get the freshest ground ginger you can find—it's great if it is still moist and almost gooey.

Yield: 6 generous servings

2 cups all purpose flour

1½ cups granulated sugar

2 tablespoons molasses

4 teaspoons lemon zest

½ cup vegetable oil

¼ cup freshly squeezed lemon juice

1 tablespoon melted butter

¾ teaspoon freshly ground ginger

1 cup yogurt

1 egg, beaten

1 teaspoon Mexican vanilla

½ teaspoon baking powder

½ teaspoon baking soda

1. Set the rack in the oven in the center position. Preheat to 350°. Butter an 8-inch square baking pan. Combine the flour, sugar, molasses, and zest in a bowl. Then add the oil, lemon juice and butter and mix well. The mixture should be crumbly. Reserve 1 cup of this mixture and set to the side.

2. Combine the remaining ingredients in another bowl to create the yogurt mixture. Create the batter by adding the yogurt mixture to the crumb mixture. Stir well.

3. Spread the batter uniformly in the bottom of the buttered pan. Sprinkle the reserved flour mixture over the top and place in the oven. Bake about 45 minutes or until a toothpick comes out clean. Cool on a rack until ready to serve.

Green Chile Harvest Lunch

❧

M E N U

New Mexico's Own Chardonnay

Green Chile-Laced Queso Fundido
with Miniature Warm Flour Tortillas

Grilled Rubbed Chicken Breast on
Baby Greens with Green Chile Dressing

Green Chile Relleno Salad
with Salsa Vinaigrette

Pumpkin Cheesecake Torte

Coffee

❧

Green chile is uniquely bountiful and popular in New Mexico, where more chiles are grown than anywhere on this continent and where more green chile is consumed per capita than anywhere!

Come join in the fun and flavor. Green chiles have an addictive taste that, once enjoyed, will never be forgotten. Roasting green chiles spread a tantalizing aroma throughout the streets of New Mexico from August into late October, when the red chile harvest begins. (They are ripe green chiles.)

This luncheon could be staged anywhere, in or out of doors. Although most any colorful table setting will work, I especially like using greens on green. Select your favorite green tablecloth or one that coordinates nicely with green, such as a yellow or gold one. Use pottery of a neutral color like beige or white and colorful glasses if you have them.

Early fall is the scene here, so use a multi-colored collection of late-blooming garden flowers such as asters and chrysanthemums. Dried grasses and flowers work well too, as does dried multi-colored corn. Of course you will need to watch the height of the centerpiece so that it doesn't hamper conversation.

MENU PLAN

One day ahead:

Parch the green chiles for all the dishes and peel them, keeping the prettiest four reserved for the salad.

Prepare the chicken breast and rub with the baste/rub.

Prepare and bake the Pumpkin Cheesecake Torte.

Prepare the dressing and vinaigrette.

One to two hours before:

Stuff the chiles for the salad.

Combine the ingredients for the fundido to prepare for heating.

One hour or less before serving time, depending on the time required, heat the grill to 450°.

Place the tortillas in a plastic bag for microwave warming or in foil for heating in a conventional oven.

Warm the plates in a 200° oven.

Grill the chicken and keep it warm.

Dress the salad just before the guests arrive.

Prepare coffee.

At serving time:

As guests arrive, serve the chardonnay.

Heat the fundido and serve with the warm tortillas.

Serve the main course—the grilled chicken and salad.

Serve the pumpkin torte with coffee if desired.

Green Chile-Laced Queso Fundido
with Miniature Warm Flour Tortillas

This border version blossoms biggest in San Antonio. Here is a variation of the original melted cheese dish or fundido, *which probably got its inspiration from the Swiss* raclette *or fondue.*

Yield: 4 servings

8 ounces mozzarella cheese
8 ounces asadero cheese
1/4 teaspoon Mexican oregano
4 green chiles, parched, peeled, and chopped (reserve 2 tablespoons or about 1/3 for the garnish)
1 tablespoon toasted piñon nuts, coarsely chopped
1 package or 8 miniature or medium-sized flour tortillas cut in halves or quarters

1. Using a small, heavy, cast-iron skillet or a cheese fondue pot, combine all the ingredients, except the reserved green chile and the tortillas, and stir to combine over a medium heat.

2. Continue to stir and cook until the cheese is uniformly melted. Meanwhile, warm the small tortillas in a plastic bag in the microwave for 30 seconds or wrap in foil and warm in a moderate oven for about 15 minutes or until warm.

3. Serve each guest two folded tortillas on a small plate. Then explain that each guest dips portions of the flour tortilla into the fundido. The fundido is best served in the pot in which it was melted, because if it cools, it gets hard and will need to be rewarmed.

Grilled Rubbed Chicken Breast on Baby Greens with Green Chile Dressing

The rub/baste on the chicken breast truly raises it above the ordinary and is rather quick and easy to make. Do be careful to evenly rub and pat it into the breast on both sides, allowing it to marinate at least an hour. Don't worry if the chile seems to stain your hands when you rub it into the breasts—chile washes right off with soap and water.

In the meantime, rinse and prepare the greens, spinning or patting them dry.

Chicken Breast Rub/Baste

Yield: 4 servings

4 cloves garlic, finely minced
2 tablespoons each pure ground mild and hot New Mexico chile
2 teaspoons freshly ground ginger
2 teaspoons ground coriander
2 teaspoons fresh lemon zest (the yellow part only—a zester works best)
2 tablespoons pure Spanish olive oil
4 half chicken breasts, boneless and skinless
Green Chile Dressing (next page)

1. Combine all the ingredients but the chicken and the oil in a shallow, nonreactive bowl that is large enough to hold the 4 chicken breasts, and then add the oil. Trim the chicken breasts of cartilage and fat. Rub the mixture evenly over the breasts, using all of it. Allow the chicken to remain in the bowl until ready to grill.

2. Preheat the grill to medium hot or 450° or heat the broiler or a heavy frying pan. Grill the chicken about 3 to 5 minutes on each side or until done. (The amount of time is dependent on the thickness of the chicken breast.) To check doneness, slice into the meatiest portion; the meat should be white, not clear or pink. Immediately remove to a cutting board and slice across the grain into ½ inch wide strips.

3. Prepare the Green Chile Dressing.

4. For each serving, place the greens on four chilled plates. Top with the sliced chicken on each. Garnish each serving with the fresh diced tomatoes and scallions. Either serve the salad dressing on the side or drizzle on each serving.

Baby Greens

Yield: 4 servings

6 cups assorted very fresh baby garden greens
1 small head radicchio
4 scallions, dark green tops removed, thinly sliced
3 roma or 2 small tomatoes, diced

Rinse the greens and radicchio, pat dry and place in a large salad bowl and chill.

Green Chile Dressing

Yield: enough to dress 4 main dish salads

⅔ cup extra virgin Spanish olive oil
¼ cup balsamic vinegar
1 tablespoon Dijon mustard
1 teaspoon sugar
2 tablespoons chopped green chile (approximately 1 parched, peeled green chile, diced)

Combine all ingredients in a liquid measuring cup and whisk together. Serve over or on the side with the above salad.

Green Chile Relleno Salad

This salad looks exactly like a lily or stylized flower, making for an attractive serving.

Yield: 4 servings

4 large green chiles, parched and peeled
4 ounces or more of Montrachet or other goat cheese or cream cheese
1 recipe Salsa Vinaigrette (recipe follows)

1. Parch and peel the chiles and set aside. Place them on a cutting board and with a sharp knife, slice the bottom two-thirds of each chile, cutting down from about 2 inches below the stem to create "petals" about ¾ inch wide that will be more pointed on each tip. (Leave the stems on and the tops whole.) Divide the cheese into 4 equal logs, stuffing each chile with the cheese. Chill 4 salad plates.

2. Prepare the Salsa Vinaigrette. To serve, place a puddle of ¼ the Salsa Vinaigrette on each plate, then arrange each chile to create a mum-like flower, spreading the cut portions apart and swirling each slightly. Serve as a salad.

Salsa Vinaigrette

2 tablespoons red wine vinegar
¼ cup extra virgin olive oil
⅓ cup Fresh Garden Salsa (see page 31)

Combine the vinegar, oil, and salsa to create the vinaigrette.

Pumpkin Cheesecake Torte

This torte is creamy and wonderful. And it's best made a day ahead!

Yield: 1 9-inch unbaked pie shell

CREAM CHEESE MIXTURE

Cream cheese mixture:
1 8-ounce package cream cheese
¹/₃ cup granulated sugar
1 teaspoon vanilla, Mexican if possible
1 egg, beaten

PUMPKIN MIXTURE:

1¹/₄ cups cooked or canned, pureed pumpkin
1 cup evaporated milk
²/₃ cup granulated sugar
2 eggs, beaten
2 teaspoons pumpkin pie spice
¹/₄ cup toasted pecans, coarsely chopped

1. Preheat the oven to 350°. Combine the cream cheese with the rest of the cream cheese mixture ingredients and beat with a mixer or blend well in a food processor.

2. Spoon the mixture into the pie shell. Combine the pumpkin mixture ingredients, using a whisk, mixer, blender, or food processor. Pour the pumpkin mixture on top of the cheese mixture. Using your finger or a rubber scraper, lightly mix through the two mixtures to marbelize them.

3. Bake for 1 hour or until the pie is done, which you can tell by jiggling it. It should be firm and an inserted knife should come out clean. Allow to cool before cutting or serving.

Quiet Scintillating Supper

✿

M E N U

Iced Champagne

Poquito Potatoes
with American Gold Caviar

Crab Quiche Mexicano

Chicory Salad with Grapefruit

Mexican Pecan-Toffee Tartlets
in Chocolate Chip Cookie Crust

Coffee

✿

Consider this almost sinfully sensuous menu when entertaining six of your nearest and dearest. Or, if you prefer, choose it to please your very own dearest, either reserving the balance of the quiche and the tartlets in the freezer, or cutting each recipe in thirds. In either case, it is a relatively simple meal to prepare, and a delight to savor in a comfortable, pretty setting. Although the soothing foods I have combined here are particularly pleasing late at night after the theater, or an evening outing of most any kind, this menu, inspired by the innovations of nouvelle cuisine, would be equally appropriate as a late Sunday brunch.

Take some extra time to create an especially beautiful setting for this supper. Select a fall colors theme if possible, or use neutral china on a gold, bittersweet, or brown cloth or placemats. For the flowers, arrange a very special centerpiece of fall foliage, mums, or dried straw flowers in fall colors with dried grasses to offset it. A tall, vertical arrangement in a clear, round vase is striking. Lay a deep orange, burgundy, dark green, or dark brown table runner down the length of the table, and decorate with additional dried grasses, tucking an occasional flower in amongst them.

MENU PLAN

Day before (or early in the day):

Prepare the potato skins and stuffing for *Poquito*
  Potatoes; refrigerate both.
Prepare the quiche and bake.
Prepare the tartlets and freeze.
Rinse the greens, prepare grapefruit sections
  and onion rings, and wrap each separately.
Prepare salad dressing.
Chill the champagne.

Within one hour of serving:

Chill the salad plates and forks.
Warm the dinner plates and saucers for potatoes.
Place the potato skins in a 350° oven 15 minutes
  before serving. Reheat the potato stuffing.
Set out the coffeemaker.

Place the quiche in the same oven, checking it as
  you remove the potato skins. (It should
  require 10 to 15 minutes more to be heated
  through. Watch carefully, however: the
  quiche should be hot, so that an inserted knife
  comes out clean and steam releases, but not
  too hot, or it will break down and become
  watery.)

At serving time:

Stuff the potato skins and serve with champagne.
Arrange the salad on the chilled plates.
Pour dressing over each and serve with the
  quiche.
Serve the dessert.

Poquito Potatoes with American Gold Caviar

You really should allow three to four per person—unless your guests have very hearty appetites, in which case allow up to six. First popularized in northern California, these elegant appetizers prove that the whole is often more than the sum of its parts.

Yield: 6 servings

18 to 24 new potatoes, 1½ to 2 inches in diameter
4 tablespoons sweet (unsalted) butter
¾ teaspoon salt
Several grinds of black pepper
½ pint sour cream
2 ounces American gold caviar

1. Preheat oven to 425°. Wash the potatoes and blot dry; butter the skins, using no more than 2 tablespoons. Place them on a baking sheet.

2. Bake 30 minutes, then squeeze gently, using a potholder to protect your hands. If they are done, the potatoes will yield to pressure and the skins will be somewhat crisp.

3. When done, allow the potatoes to cool slightly; cut the top third off each. Using a sharp knife, cut about ¼ inch in from the skin and scoop out contents of each potato. Add the remaining 2 tablespoons of butter, the salt, pepper, and a scoop of the sour cream and beat until the potatoes are fluffy.

4. If serving immediately, return the skins to the hot oven and bake about 20 minutes more to really crisp the skins. If preparing the potatoes earlier in the day or even a day or two before, refrigerate; then wait to crisp the skins in a 350° oven just before you are ready to serve.

5. For refrigerated potatoes and stuffing, heat the skins as above and reheat the mashed potatoes separately. If using a microwave, cover and heat for a minute, then rotate a quarter turn, continuing until hot. If using a double boiler, place in covered top pan over the boiling water and heat for 10 to 15 minutes, or until hot.

6. To serve, spoon the potato filling back into the shells, dividing it evenly among them. Then top each with the remaining sour cream and garnish with caviar. Serve very warm on warm saucers. If serving informally from a buffet, place them on a heated serving tray and encourage guests to eat them with their hands.

Crab Quiche Mexicano

My guests, and especially my daughter Amy, have always been so fond of this dish that they never cease to request repeat appearances. Prepare it in advance and reheat, or, because it can be held uncooked a few hours, assemble the quiche, go to the theater, and bake just before serving.

Yield: 6 servings

3 wheat tortillas, 8 to 9 inch diameter

$1/4$ cup sweet (unsalted) butter or lard

4 fresh green chiles, parched, peeled, and seeds removed (see page 17)

$3/4$ cup each grated Monterey Jack and cheddar (yellow type) cheeses, mixed

1 can ($6^1/2$ ounces) flaked crab, or $3/4$ cup fresh or frozen

3 chopped green onions (scallions), including some of the tops

1 tablespoon chopped cilantro, optional

4 large eggs

$1^1/2$ cups half-and-half

A few grinds of black pepper

$1/2$ teaspoon salt

$3/4$ teaspoon caribe (crushed dried red chile)

2 or more green chiles, parched, peeled, deseeded, and chopped (see page 17), optional

$1/2$ cup sour cream, optional

1. Select a shallow round cake pan that is the same diameter as the tortillas, so that a whole one will just fit in the bottom. Cut 2 of the tortillas so that the curved outside edge comes to the top of the baking pan. Cut enough to encircle the inside of the pan completely, usually five. Melt the butter or lard in a heavy skillet and fry all the tortillas until lightly browned on each side and drain on paper towels.

2. Arrange the whole fried tortilla in the bottom of the pan, then stand the cut pieces of tortilla around the rim of the baking pan, creating a crust. Place the whole green chiles in a smooth, uniform layer over the fried tortilla on the bottom of the baking pan. Top with 1 cup of the grated cheeses, the crab, scallions, and the cilantro (or the cilantro can be served on the side).

3. Beat the eggs with the half-and-half, pepper, and salt. Pour over the crab mixture, top with the remaining $1/2$ cup of grated cheese, and sprinkle with the caribe. If baking later, cover and refrigerate.

4. When ready to bake, place in a 375° oven for 30 to 40 minutes, or until puffed and lightly browned. Serve with additional green chiles and sour cream.

Chicory Salad with Grapefruit

Both tart and light, this salad is an ideal counterpoint to any seafood, chicken, or pork main dish—as well as to quiches.

Yield: 6 servings

1 head of curly chicory
2 large red grapefruits, peeled and seeded
6 thin slices of a large red salad onion
½ cup salad oil
¼ cup white wine vinegar
1 tablespoon honey

1. Using chilled plates, arrange the chicory leaves on each. Divide the grapefruit into sections, carefully cutting away the membrane (no white from the membrane should remain). On each plate, arrange grapefruit sections in an artful pinwheel design over the chicory.

2. Top each with the separated onion rings. Combine the oil, wine vinegar, and honey and drizzle over each.

Mexican Pecan-Toffee Tartlets
in Chocolate Chip Cookie Crust

Who doesn't like chocolate chip cookies? Judging from the thriving cookie establishments and cookie wars announced by the trade, we know they're a hit, and when combined with pecan-studded coffee-toffee ice cream, the result is a rich blend of flavors that no dessert lover can resist.

Yield: 6 servings

24 small or 12 medium-size chocolate chip cookies
4 tablespoons sweet (unsalted) butter, melted
1 pint coffee ice cream (select a good, rich one)
1 toffee candy bar, 4-ounce size
½ cup very coarsely chopped pecan halves
½ pint heavy whipping cream
3 tablespoons vanilla-scented sugar (made by storing sugar with a broken piece of vanilla bean)
½ cup thick, rich chocolate fudge sauce

1. Using a food processor, blender, or a rolling pin, crush the cookies until finely crumbled. Meanwhile, melt the butter.

2. Butter the insides of 6 small soufflé cups, or any other suitable small serving dishes. Combine remaining butter with the cookie crumbs in a bowl.

3. Divide the mixture evenly among the 6 cups, and then press it firmly into them. Freeze.

4. Soften the ice cream by scooping it into a mixing bowl and letting it set a few minutes, then process in a food processor or mixer.

5. Crush the toffee bar in the processor or with a rolling pin, until it is in chunks about ½ inch across, not too fine. Add to the ice cream along with ⅓ cup of the pecans. Process or mix until just combined so as not to overly crush the candy and the nuts. Divide among the cookie crusts, leaving the surface of each somewhat uneven and interesting looking as you would frosting.

6. Whip the cream with the vanilla sugar.

7. Divide the chocolate fudge sauce among each of the tarts, drizzling it in a swirl in the center of each, allowing some of the ice cream filling around the edges to show.

8. Top each with a dollop of the whipped cream. If you have too much, place the extra in dollops on a cookie sheet covered with wax paper and freeze for later garnishing for drinks or desserts.

9. Sprinkle reserved pecan pieces over the top of the cream. Freeze until serving time.

New Mexico Buffet

M E N U

*Hot Spicy Chicken Wings
with Creamy Salsa Verde*

Santa Fe Lasagna

Fall Squash Medley

Bear Paw Bread

Sweet Butter

Zinfandel

*Figs with Port Wine and
Mexican Goat Cheese*

Coffee

The cozy feelings of fall—the cooler mornings and evenings and harvest moon at night—seem to call for the warmth of spicy foods. This menu is made to order for fall appetites.

The Bear Paw Bread is extraordinarily good when freshly baked. Try to plan your time to bake the bread shortly before serving time, but if scheduling becomes a problem, French bread or most any peasant hearth-type bread can be substituted. Better yet, reheat a previously frozen loaf of Bear Paw Bread.

The Santa Fe Lasagna is one of my favorite inventions. It is a dish that can be assembled whenever you have the time, set aside in the refrigerator for up to 5 days, and baked just before serving. It also freezes for up to 3 months.

The spicy chicken wing appetizer is an increasingly popular treat, and though it requires last minute frying, it is worth the extra effort. In fact, you will probably be able to recruit helpers for the frying. The salad and figs are very quickly assembled, rounding out this menu with a simple but elegant grace note.

For decor, aim for a New Mexican accent: clay pottery and baskets for serving, terra cotta tiles or dishes, and earthy russets to browns for the table linens. Cactus or evergreen boughs make a complementary centerpiece, or, for an unusual touch, try a Southwestern Indian sculpture such as a storyteller or corn maiden.

Day before, early in the day, or several days in advance:

Prepare the lasagna for baking and refrigerate.

Make the bread dough, planning the risings so that the bread will be baked about 30 minutes before serving dinner—allow at least 4½ hours to be on the safe side. If it has risen to the point where it needs to be baked, and it's too far ahead of dinner, you can keep it in the refrigerator.

Coat the chicken wings and freeze.

Up to one or two hours before:

Prepare the Creamy Salsa Verde and chill.

Bake the bread.

Heat the oil for the chicken about 20 minutes ahead.

Prepare the vegetables and stew the squash.

Fill a favorite butter dish and allow the butter to come to room temperature.

Set out the coffeepot.

Arrange the figs on a platter and keep at room temperature. Set out the cheese on a board or server.

Put the lasagna in the oven just before the guests arrive.

At serving time:

Fry the chicken wings and serve with the salsa.

Assemble the salad. Serve with the lasagna, Bear Paw Bread, and sweet butter.

Serve the Figs with Port Wine and Mexican Goat Cheese.

Serve coffee.

Hot Spicy Chicken Wings with Creamy Salsa Verde

Based on the famous buffalo chicken wings, this zippy snack was developed when I was looking for something unusual for an appetizer. I was inspired by Dean Small, director of the delightful array of food shops and eateries in the Heartland Market in the Crown Center Complex in Kansas City, Missouri. He enthusiastically shared an idea for a similar dish he had created for the market's American Café Restaurant.

Yield: 6 servings

½ cup masa harina (if not available, substitute yellow cornmeal)
1½ teaspoons ground cumin
2 tablespoons ground pure hot chile, New Mexico type
½ teaspoon salt
½ cup all-purpose flour
1 cup milk
24 chicken wings
1 quart vegetable oil
Creamy Salsa Verde (see page 32)

1. Combine the masa harina with the cumin, chile, and salt in a shallow bowl. Place the flour and milk in separate bowls.

2. Rinse and pick any pinfeathers off the chicken wings. Blot dry. Dip each wing in the milk, then the flour, the milk again, and then the masa harina mixture. Set on a cookie sheet covered with wax paper. The chicken wings can be frozen at this point for up to 3 months.

3. If cooking immediately, heat the oil in a deep-fat fryer, preferably with a thermostatic control set at 375°. If no thermostat is available, then use a heavy pot and a candy thermometer. While the oil heats, place the wings in the freezer to firm up. (This makes the coating cling better throughout the frying process and the meat is juicier.)

4. Fry two to three wings at a time, until each is golden, about 3 minutes each, then drain on paper towels and keep warm in a low oven. Serve warm, with the salsa alongside.

Santa Fe Lasagna

What dish could find greater favor with diners than one that is the happy marriage of two terrific cuisines? I set about creating a version of that perennial favorite, lasagna, using chorizo, *sausage sparked with hot New Mexico chiles, instead of Italian sausage. A generous amount of the ubiquitous cheeses of the Southwest—Monterey Jack and cheddar—take the place of mozzarella in this very flavorful entrée, and tortillas replace noodles.*

Yield: 6 servings

¹/₂ cup vegetable oil, optional (see Note)

12 corn tortillas

4 cups (about 1 pound) grated full cream yellow cheddar cheese and Monterey Jack cheese, mixed

1 cup red Spanish onion, diced

1 pound chorizo (see note), removed from its casings and chopped, cooked, and drained

15 ounces ricotta cheese

3 cups half-and-half

1. If frying, heat the oil in a heavy skillet. Arrange paper towels over paper plates for draining the tortillas. Lightly fry each until soft. Drain well.

2. Using some of the oil, lightly oil a 9 x 13-inch baking dish.

3. Place 3 tortillas in the dish, then a layer of grated cheese, onions, cooked *chorizo*, and ricotta. Repeat with 3 more tortillas, using about one fourth of each ingredient for each layer, until you have four layers. Pour the half-and-half evenly over the dish. (The lasagna can be refrigerated at this point, or frozen.)

4. Bake in a 350° oven for 30 minutes, or until bubbly.

Note: For greater convenience and less fat, omit frying the tortillas. If *chorizo* is difficult to find in your local markets, you can make it at home, or alter hot Italian sausage according to the directions included in the Chorizo and Piñon-Stuffed Loin of Pork on page 165.

Fall Squash Medley

Pueblo Indians prepare wild squash, which is pale green and gourdlike, by stewing it together with the vegetables they have on hand. Often it is combined with corn, tomatoes, and onion.

Yield: 6 servings

2 teaspoons extra virgin olive oil, preferably Spanish

¹/₂ medium onion, sliced thinly into rings

2 cloves garlic, minced

3 medium zucchini or a combination of green and yellow squash, thinly sliced into rounds

2 fresh tomatoes, peeled and coarsely cubed into about ³/₄ inch dice

¹/₂ teaspoon salt

¹/₂ teaspoon ground Mexican oregano

1. Using a heavy saucepan, heat the oil, then saute the onion and garlic until almost clear. Stir in the squash and tomatoes and cover.

2. Cook over medium low heat until squash is tender. Add salt if desired and Mexican oregano. Taste and adjust seasonings. Serve warm.

Bear Paw Bread

This traditional New Mexican Pueblo bread is baked and sold by Indians in front of the Palace of the Governors in Santa Fe, as well as at little roadside stands and at fairs, fiestas, and rodeos. It's wonderful freshly baked, oozing with sweet butter and topped with local cactus honeys or jams.

Yield: 1 loaf

¹/₂ package dry yeast (approximately 1¹/₂ teaspoons)
¹/₄ cup warm water
Pinch of sugar
¹/₄ teaspoon lard
¹/₄ teaspoon honey
¹/₄ teaspoon salt
2¹/₂ or more cups all-purpose flour

1. Sprinkle the yeast over the warm water and add the pinch of sugar.

2. Combine all the remaining ingredients except the flour in the bottom of a large mixing bowl and stir to dissolve. When the yeast mixture is cooled to room temperature and bubbly, combine with the lard/honey mixture.

3. Add the flour, 1 cup at a time. Stir briskly to make a bubbly sponge. Then add flour only until a stiff dough results. Do not add more—if not all of it is used, save it to the side. When the dough is too stiff to continue stirring, turn it out onto a floured board. Knead until smooth and elastic, about 10 minutes or so.

4. Place the dough in a clean, oiled bowl, covering it with a damp towel. Then place in a warm place, free from drafts.

5. When the dough has doubled, in about 1 hour, turn it out on the floured board and roll into a flat disk about 8 inches in diameter. Place on a lightly oiled cookie sheet. Fold over, making certain you leave about two inches of the bottom layer overlapping—similar to a stollen. Placing your palm on the center of the folded edge toward you, press it away from you and pull the edges toward you to form a broad "U" shape. Using a sharp knife, cutting through both layers, slash once about 2 inches from each outside edge to form a claw effect on the outside of the bread.

6. Cover with a damp towel and set aside until doubled, about 1 hour.

7. Meantime, preheat the oven to 350° and place a pan of boiling water on the lower shelf. Place the bread on the shelf above and bake for 1 hour, or until it is very slightly brown and sounds hollow when thumped. (This bread is traditionally baked in hornos—adobe ovens—using piñon wood coals for heat.)

❈   ❈   ❈

Fresh Figs with Port Wine and Mexican Goat Cheese

Although figs are popular as a lawn shrub in New Mexico, the best are grown in the mountainous area of the southern part of the state. I've always savored Cloudcroft figs (Cloudcroft is a resort tucked in the mountains near Ruidoso) as something special, and in this simple dessert their unmatchable sweetness can be enjoyed with a pair of ideal complements. Lacking figs or if you are not fond of them, substitute freshly harvested apples.

Yield: 6 servings

36 fresh ripe figs
1 roll (4 ounces) each Mexican goat cheese, if available, and Montrachet
1 fifth port wine

1. Rinse the figs and set on pretty crystal or simple clear glass plates or any favorite dessert plates. Do this ahead so the figs are at room temperature.

2. Place the cheeses on a cheese board.

3. To serve, pour the port and give each guest a plate of figs. They are delightful eaten together with the goat cheese.

Note: Some people also like to serve a simple water cracker.

Microwave Mexican for Busy Evenings

❧

M E N U

Halloween Soup

Picadillo Rice

Spicy Pork Chops Rancher's Style

Marinated Baby Green Bean Salad

*Warm Wheat Tortillas
with Fresh Oregano Butter*

Lime Ice

Zinfandel

Coffee

❧

When you find yourself with a tight schedule yet wish to cook for guests, this menu can be cooked and served in 30 minutes if you use a microwave oven, provided the soup is made, the Lime Ice, and the Marinated Baby Green Bean Salad have been prepared in advance. If cooking conventionally, allow 1 hour of preparation time; instructions are given in each of the recipes for cooking either way.

For this time-saving menu set the table in gay bright colors with a simple centerpiece of seasonal flowers—chrysanthemums are ideal in the fall—or a bowl of fruit or vegetables.

You may wish to serve some thin, crisp cookies alongside the Lime Ice.

MENU PLAN

Day before:

Prepare the Lime Ice. (Refrigerate 2 hours
before serving.)
Prepare the Marinated Baby Green Bean Salad.

Thirty minutes before:

Prepare the pork chops.
Warm the dinner plates.
Warm the soup.
Prepare the Fresh Oregano Butter.
Wrap tortillas in two foil packets of 6 each.

Prepare the Picadillo Rice.
Scoop out servings of Lime Ice, placing them in
sherbet glasses, then return them to the
freezer.

At serving time:

Warm the tortillas.
Arrange the salad on lettuce leaves.
Serve the pork chops on hot plates with the rice,
tortillas, and oregano butter, and the salad.
Serve the Lime Ice.

Halloween Soup

After Halloween, the pumpkin shell often goes begging or just into pulp for pies later. How about making this soup with part of the leftover pumpkin? Pumpkin and winter squash were all originally cultivated by the Native North Americans and are very popular in the Southwest.

You can make this soup ahead and freeze for at least three months.

Yield: 6 servings

5 cups vegetable stock
1 small onion, chopped
1 clove garlic, minced
2 leaves fresh sage (1/2 teaspoon dried)
3 cups pumpkin, cut in chunks
1 1/2 cups evaporated skim milk
1 teaspoon crushed caribe chile

1. Place vegetable stock in a pot and add onion, garlic, sage, and pumpkin and simmer covered until done—about 30 to 40 minutes.

2. Puree in a food processor or blender and add the milk. Taste and adjust seasonings and place back in the pot and simmer for another 10 minutes or until flavors blend. Serve in warm bowls. Garnish with sprinkle of caribe chile.

Note: The soup can be frozen after pureeing and then heated just to serve.

❊   ❊   ❊

Picadillo Rice

When you've cooked one too many portions of simple white rice, try this delicious southwestern version of a pilaf. It's quick to assemble, as you add the flavorings after the rice has cooked.

Yield: 6 servings

3 cups water
1 1/2 teaspoons salt
1 1/2 cups rice
2 tablespoons sweet (unsalted) butter
1 teaspoon whole coriander, crushed
1/3 cup dark raisins
1/3 cup slivered almonds
1/8 teaspoon ground cloves
1/4 teaspoon ground cinnamon

1. Using a medium saucepan, bring the water to a boil with the salt. Add the rice and butter and stir, then cover and reduce heat. Set a timer for 15 minutes.

2. Meanwhile, prepare, measure, and combine the remaining ingredients. When the rice is done, stir in the mixture, reserving 2 tablespoons for garnish. Cover and set aside to fluff for about 5 minutes, or until ready to serve alongside the pork chops. Garnish with the remaining spice mixture.

Spicy Pork Chops Rancher's Style

This flavorful, quick entrée can be made on top of the range if you don't have a microwave oven. If you have some on hand, use previously cooked or frozen Ranchero Sauce instead of the onions, tomatoes, green chiles and garlic.

Yield: 6 servings

2 tablespoons extra virgin olive oil, preferably Spanish

2 cups chopped Spanish onions (2 large)

1 can (28 ounces) whole peeled tomatoes with their juice

2 to 3 large New Mexico green chiles, parched (see page 17), peeled, and chopped (¹/₂ cup) or 2 ounces canned chopped green chiles

2 garlic cloves, minced

1 teaspoon ground comino (cumin)

6 large, well-trimmed 2-inch-thick loin pork chops (2 to 2¹/₂ pounds)

1. If using the microwave oven, use an 8 x 10-inch glass baking dish. Coat the bottom evenly with the olive oil. A rubber scraper will work fine for this. Add the onion, cover with waxed paper, and process on high heat for about 2 minutes, or until the onion begins to sizzle and becomes somewhat clear. If it hasn't after 2 minutes, stir, rotate, and cook another minute. If not using a microwave oven, place the oil in a large deep frying pan that has a tight-fitting cover. Add the onion and sauté until clear, about 5 minutes.

2. If cooking in the microwave oven, add the tomatoes, green chiles, and garlic. Cover with waxed paper and process for 3 minutes, stirring and rotating once. Taste and add salt, if desired, and more chiles if a hotter sauce is desired. If cooking in the frying pan, add the tomatoes, chiles, and garlic and cook for 11 to 15 minutes, or until the flavors combine.

3. For the microwave or the frying pan, place the pork chops evenly across the sauce, spooning about half of it over the tops of the chops. Cover with wax paper for the microwave and process for 15 minutes at full power, turning three or four times, spooning sauce over the top and rotating each time. Keep covered with the wax paper. If cooking in a skillet, cover and cook over medium-low heat for 40 to 60 minutes, spooning sauce over every 5 minutes or so. For either method, insert a sharp knife next to the bone to determine doneness. If the meat is slightly pink, cook another few minutes until the internal temperature is 165°. The meat should look pinkish-white. Serve piping hot on heated plates with the Picadillo Rice.

Marinated Baby Green Bean Salad

This simple, fresh, very green salad is perfect for any quick meal. If you have a bit more time, though, prepare it a day before you plan to serve, and the marinade will have an even richer flavor.

Yield: 6 servings

1½ pounds green beans
2 cups water
½ teaspoon salt
1 cup salad oil
⅓ cup cider vinegar
1 teaspoon caribe, or other crushed dried red chile
2 very thin slices of red Spanish onion
6 large leafy lettuce leaves

1. Clean and trim the stems from the green beans. Boil the water with the salt. Add the beans and simmer, covered, for 5 to 8 minutes—only until the color deepens and the beans are slightly tender, yet still crisp. If cooking in the microwave oven, place in an ovenproof glass pie plate or baking dish and sprinkle with salt. Do not add the water. Just cover with plastic wrap and process on high speed for 2 minutes, rotate a quarter turn, then process another minute. Check for doneness. If not tender enough, process another minute, or until done.

2. Meanwhile, place the oil, vinegar, and caribe in a wide-mouthed jar and shake well.

3. Drain the beans and add to the jar along with the onion slices. Set aside and allow to marinate 2 to 3 hours, or even overnight. Shake periodically to distribute the dressing evenly. Serve on lettuce leaves.

Warm Wheat Tortillas with Fresh Oregano Butter

Herb or citrus-zest butters provide a change of pace from wheat tortillas or other southwestern breads. For freshest flavor prepare this just before serving, but if timing is a problem, it can be made as much as a day ahead.

Yield: enough to serve 6 or more

12 wheat tortillas

¼ pound sweet (unsalted) butter, softened

1½ teaspoons coarsely chopped fresh Mexican oregano leaves, or ¾ teaspoon dried (or ground)

1. Place the tortillas in two plastic bags in the microwave for 1 minute and remove to a napkin-lined basket. Or heat in foil "pockets" in a 350° oven for 20 minutes or until hot.

2. Combine the butter with the oregano in a small bowl, then place in a small dish just large enough to hold the butter. Smooth the top and set aside.

3. To serve, I suggest guests butter their tortillas and eat them rolled.

Lime Ice

Here is a dessert so refreshing you'll want to prepare it for nearly every meal. I like to make this a few days in advance and freeze it, then let it mellow 2 to 3 hours in the refrigerator before serving. Accompany with thin, crisp cookies alongside, if you wish.

Yield: 2½ quarts

4¾ cups water

2¼ cups sugar

3 cups freshly squeezed lime juice

¼ cup freshly squeezed lemon juice

1 tablespoon lime zest, minced

1. Combine the water and sugar in a 2-quart saucepan. Simmer for 5 minutes to create a simple syrup.

2. Remove from the heat and chill.

3. Pour the chilled mixture into the canister of your ice cream maker. Add lime juice, lemon juice, and the lime zest. Mix with a wooden spoon or spatula.

4. Follow the directions for your ice cream maker to create a firm ice. Freeze until firm 2 to 3 hours before serving, then put in the refrigerator. To serve, form into balls with an ice cream scoop, dipping it into warm water between scoops. I like to serve it in footed sherbet glasses, but wine glasses—especially the tulip or globular types—will also work well. Freeze again before serving.

V ❈ Winter

New Year's Day Country Brunch
A Winter Fireside Lunch
Old El Paso Border Dinner
Apres Ski
Late Night's Pleasure

New Year's Day Country Brunch

❦

M E N U

Chorizo Chalupitas

*Rolled Ham 'n Chile Omelet Pinwheel
with Mushroom Ratatouille*

Tropical Fruit-Stuffed Pineapple

Champagne

Coffee

❦

This is a perfect brunch to serve by the fireside in a cozy country cabin. I first served it as a toast to the New Year, and it was a winner. The foods are not complicated to cook, and you need pay special attention only to the omelet instructions. Ready the base for the *chalupitas* the day before, and the rest of the preparations will require only about an hour. (*Chalupas* are the canoe-like boats in the lake gardens of Mexico City; *chalupitas* are small, boat-shaped appetizers.)

Select a colorful tablecloth and place it over a large, low coffee table in front of your couch before the fireplace. Or, set a quilt on your dining room table with a complement of bright print napkins folded in fan shapes and stuffed into large wine goblets. Complete the table with a winter bouquet of multicolored mums or other favorite flowers, or fruit and nuts.

MENU PLAN

Day before:

Fry the *chalupitas.*
Chill the champagne.

One hour before:

Prepare the pineapple and fruits.
Prepare the ratatouille.
Cook the *chorizo* and warm the tortilla flutes
30 minutes before serving; assemble the
chalupitas and garnish the platter.

Prepare the pan and ingredients for the omelet.
Set out the coffeepot.

At serving time:

Bake the omelet while serving the *chalupitas*
with the champagne.
Roll and serve the omelet with the ratatouille,
and serve more champagne.
Arrange the Tropical Fruit-Stuffed Pineapple
and serve with the coffee.

Chorizo Chalupitas

Chalupas are *perhaps one of the most liberally interpreted dishes in Mexican fast food operations. You'll find everything from an open-face salad in its own edible bowl (which should be called a* tostado compuesto) *to a simple, fried flat corn or wheat tortilla layered with taco types of fillings. Traditionally, Mexican* chalupas *were made in the Mexico City area as a treat for the children while their mothers cooked—an origin somewhat similar to that of tacos further north.*

I developed these as an innovative twist to the traditional. Chorizo is a wonderful breakfast meat, yet can be far too spicy for some unless it is combined with other ingredients—hence, this tasty little appetizer. Instead of the traditional masa "canoe" shape for the chalupas, *I recommend using small corn tortillas—half size, if available (3 inches in diameter). Otherwise, use the 6-inch size. You can make these the day or evening before and reheat and serve.*

Yield: 12 appetizers

2 quarts cooking oil
1 dozen 3-inch or ½ dozen 6-inch corn tortillas
¾ pound (12 ounces) chorizo sausage, preferably the New Mexican or Mexican-American type
8 ounces sour cream
1½ cups thinly shredded iceberg lettuce
½ cup halved black olives
2 tablespoons coarsely chopped fresh cilantro, optional

1. Heat the oil in an electric deep-fat fryer to 375°, or in a 5-quart heavy Dutch oven using a deep-fat frying thermometer to maintain the proper temperature. Meanwhile, if using the 3-inch tortillas, find a 6-ounce juice can and using a beverage opener, punch three holes evenly spaced around the top and three more alternating between the top ones on the vertical side adjacent to the top holes. This will create a frying form. If using the 6-inch tortillas, cut each in half and curl around your finger overlapping the ends to create a flute or cylindrical shape; secure with a toothpick.

2. For the 3-inch size, place one tortilla at a time on the surface of the oil and immediately plunge it into the fat, using tongs to hold the punched end of the can down on the center of the tortilla. Fry until the bubbles subside and the tortilla is crisp and bubbly. For the 6-inch size, fry the flutes, holding them with tongs to be certain they are completely immersed, until they are crisp. Drain well on a cooling rack covered with absorbent paper towels.

3. About 30 minutes before serving, remove the casings from the *chorizos* and coarsely chop the meat. Fry over low heat, stirring frequently to be certain it is uniformly fried and crumbled. Drain on absorbent toweling, discarding the fat.

4. Reheat the fried tortillas in a 350° oven for 10 minutes and fill each with the crumbled *chorizo*. Top with sour cream, and place on an attractive platter. Garnish each with shredded lettuce, using the balance to garnish the platter. Top each with a few slices of olive and a sprinkle of cilantro, if desired.

Rolled Ham 'n Chile Omelet Pinwheel with Mushroom Ratatouille

Gorgeous is the only word to describe this whirl of brilliant color. A pinwheel omelet is one of those dishes that are actually fun to make, and once you've mastered its techniques, there is no limit to the variety of fillings. The major trick is buttering the wax paper or heavy wrapping paper generously enough; otherwise, what should be a lovely fluff of baked omelet loses its muscle immediately and becomes very skinny and scruffy looking. Be certain to make the ratatouille ahead of time for serving alongside.

Plan carefully so that the omelet, once done, can be served immediately. Have the eggs separated, the pan ready and the fillings laid out in advance. Then allow 20 to 25 minutes to prepare the omelet and bake, roll, and serve it.

Yield: 6 servings

12 extra large very fresh eggs, separated
12 thin slices of cooked ham, approximately
*   4 inches square (about 1/2 pound)*
3/4 teaspoon salt
A few grinds of black pepper
6 large New Mexico green chiles (can be frozen),
*   parched, peeled, and coarsely chopped*
*   (see page 17)*
6 large red leaf lettuce leaves, rinsed and drained

1. Preheat the oven to 350°. Prepare a 10 x 14-inch jelly roll pan or cookie sheet with a raised rim by generously buttering the pan, then cutting a piece of wax or greased butcher paper to cover the bottom of the pan precisely. Generously butter the top of the paper.

2. Beat the egg whites until very stiff and dry, using an electric mixer. Add the salt and pepper to the yolks and beat with a whisk until thick and lemon colored. Then fold together, carefully blending the two, and retaining as much air as possible—the mixture should stand in definite peaks. Portion out the mixture, dividing it into four piles in the corners of the pan. Working gently with a spatula, smooth off the four piles to a single omlet of uniform thickness, making certain that the mixture is smoothed to all sides of the pan. Air pockets will make for a ragged-appearing edge.

3. Place in the center of the preheated oven. (Also, place six serving plates in the oven.) Bake 15 to 20 minutes. Place the ham in a pan in the oven to heat while the omelet is baking, and place a heatproof bowl of thawed green chiles in the oven. When the omelet is done, a sharp knife or toothpick will come out clean. As soon as the omelet is done, place it on a wire cooling rack. Using a sharp knife, cut around the outside edges of the omelet and lift it, on its piece of waxed paper, onto the cooling rack. Add a layer of the ham, spreading it out to cover the top of the omelet. Sprinkle the green chile uniformly over the top.

4. Begin to roll by lifting up the long side next to the edge and rolling like a jelly roll, gently pressing the omelet down and removing the waxed paper as you roll. Sometimes I like to have a nimble-fingered helper assist with this. Continue until you have rolled the omelet into one large, long roll. Do be very careful not to rip or tear the omelet as this will destroy the overall appearance. Slice crosswise into six pinwheel servings. Place each immediately on a warmed plate, garnishing with a lettuce leaf. Add a ribbon of the warmed ratatouille over each and serve the extra alongside.

Variation: Place the warm ratatouille on each plate and top with the omelet serving.

Mushroom Ratatouille

A lovely, flavorful topping that is really quite simple to make. For generous appetites or dedicated sauce appreciators, you may wish to double this recipe, as it is lovely cold or hot tucked into omelets, as a topping for hamburgers, or even in salads.

Yield: 6 servings

2 tablespoons sweet (unsalted) butter

1 pound large button mushrooms, cleaned and thinly sliced into half-moons, leaving the stems on

1/2 cup finely chopped Spanish onion

2 large fresh or canned tomatoes, peeled and chopped

2 teaspoons chopped fresh thyme, or 1 teaspoon dried

2 teaspoons chopped fresh Mexican oregano, or 1 teaspoon dried

6 leaves fresh purple sage, chopped, or 1 teaspoon dried, crumbled

A few grinds of black pepper

1/2 teaspoon salt

1. Melt the butter in a large heavy skillet. Add the thinly sliced mushrooms and cook and stir until they have lost their water and started to brown. Add the chopped onion and cook and stir until it becomes clear.

2. Add the remaining ingredients and cook and stir until a thick sauce results. This should not take very long—about 10 minutes or so. Taste and adjust seasonings and keep warm. Serve warm over or under the omelet and on the side.

Tropical Fruit-Stuffed Pineapple

For the prettiest servings, slice the pineapple lengthwise into boats, following my suggested cutting directions. Be certain to select a very juicy, ripe, symmetrically shaped fruit. You can tell if a pineapple is ripe when it has a fragrant aroma, thumps hollowly, and its green top leaves pull out easily. Try to find a fruit with attractive leaves, and do not remove more than one or two to test for ripeness.

Yield: 6 servings

1 very large pineapple

1 mango, peeled and cut into half circles

1 papaya, preferably the watermelon or pink type, peeled, then cut into squares

1 pint red ripe strawberries, left whole (if not available, substitute red seedless grapes)

12 fresh orange or lemon leaves, optional

1. To prepare the pineapple, select a large, sharp cutting knife or an electric knife (about the only time I really like to use one). Hold the pineapple upright by the top and slice down through the leaves and the flesh, cutting all the way down to make two halves. Cut each half lengthwise into three equal parts.

2. Next, starting at the base of each sixth, cut the flesh evenly away from the rind, cutting close enough to the rind to get a nice deep, fleshy portion, but without too many eyes. Cut each in two equal lengthwise parts, then cut into ¾-inch-wide crosswise slices.

3. Create zigzags of pineapple slices by pushing alternating slices of pineapple, one to the left about an inch, the next to the right about an inch. Then artistically scatter the tropical fruits and strawberries over the pineapple. Garnish with leaves if available.

A Winter Fireside Lunch

⁂

M E N U

Hot Spiced Cabernet

Chile-Rubbed Tenderloin Medallions

Individual Corn Chipotle Flans

Spinach Salad with Jicama and Piñon Laced with Raspberry Vinaigrette

Hot, Hot Frosted Fudge Brownies

Zinfandel

Cappuccino

⁂

This hearty, highly flavored luncheon just begs for a fireside setting. Even if your floor plan does not normally allow for the table to be in front of the fireplace, use your dining room table as a buffet or move an occasional table to the front of the fireplace.

If you don't have a fireplace, you can still enjoy this lunch. It is a wonderful idea for a cozy lunch anytime—say Valentine's Day.

Use a wintry table covering such as heavy corduroy or terrycloth. Dark colors like burgundy, deep forest green, or navy blue are best. Use plates that look well on the table covering. If possible, select a romantic or antique type of pattern, such as Currier and Ives or Ironstone. A selection of ripe fruit and nuts would make an attractive centerpiece.

Day before:

Prepare the brownies and bake. When cool,
frost them. Chill.

Prepare the hot spiced wine.

Prepare the beef rub.

Prepare the flans.

Make the salad dressing, rinse and spin dry the
spinach and place in a salad bowl. Toast the
piñon nuts and chop.

Two hours ahead:

Rub the filet with the rub mixture.

Peel and dice the jícama and place in water.

Warm the flans along with the plates in a
200° oven.

Warm the wine.

Thirty minutes before serving, if only one oven,
remove the plates and flans and cover to keep
warm. Preheat the oven to 450° for roasting
the meat.

Slice the brownies and remove to a serving plate.

Prepare the coffee and warm milk for cappuccino.

At serving time:

Serve the hot wine.

Toss the salad with the drained jícama, piñons
and dressing.

Remove the flans and warm the dinner plates.

Slice and serve the beef.

Serve the salad with the beef and flan.

Make the cappuccino and serve with the plate
of brownies.

Hot Spiced Cabernet

Warm, spicy wine has long been known for its warming capabilities—just ask any skier. If you can get canela, *the Mexican cinnamon, by all means, do. It has a more intense flavor that releases faster, making it preferable here.*

Yield: 4 servings

1 fifth Cabernet Sauvignon
½ cup sugar
¼ teaspoon ground Mexican cinnamon
¼ teaspoon ground allspice
¼ teaspoon ground cloves

⅛ teaspoon freshly grated nutmeg
4 canela (cinnamon) sticks, optional

Pour the wine into a porcelain or stainless steel pan and add all the remaining ingredients. Simmer together very lightly only until the sugar dissolves. Serve in warm mugs or Irish coffee glasses with a cinnamon stick thrust into each.

Chile-Rubbed Tenderloin Medallions

Beef is truly enhanced with a chile rub—a very Texan idea. Actually the process was probably learned from the Indians, who used chile on beef to "cure" it when they dried it for jerky. Filet is really hard to beat any way you prepare it, but this way just might become a favorite.

Yield: 4 servings

2 tablespoons ground hot or mild pure
*   New Mexican chile*
3 garlic cloves, minced
1½ teaspoon coarse salt (table salt is fine)
2 tablespoons freshly ground black or
*   green peppercorns*
2 tablespoon granulated sugar
2 teaspoons freshly ground cumin
1 2-pound beef tenderloin

1. Combine all the ingredients except the beef to make the chile rub. Trim the beef of any excess fat and evenly coat the beef with the rub, patting it in uniformly around the edges. Set aside at room temperature for about 2 hours.

2. About 30 minutes before you are ready to serve, preheat the oven to 450°. Place the beef on a rack in an open baking pan—preferably one that is easy to clean—or line it with foil. Place the beef in the oven on a medium rack position.

3. Roast the beef for about 20 minutes or to desired doneness. Rare to medium is best for this cut. The meat is done when internal temperature reaches 140° to 150° and the meat yields easily when pressed with your thumb. Remove to the counter. Quickly warm the plates under hot water and dry, or warm them in the oven. Slice the beef into ½ inch or thicker slices and place them, sliced side up, on the warmed plates. If any pan juices collect, spoon a bit over each slice.

Individual Chipotle Corn Flans

The smokiness of the chipotles *(smoked jalapeños) really settles into the corn and makes a compatible flavor combination with the beef.*

Yield: 4 3-ounce servings

2 to 3 dried chipotles
1 teaspoon apple cider vinegar
1 tablespoon sweet (unsalted) butter, plus enough
*   to butter the baking dishes*
1 cup milk
6 ounces or ³/₄ cup cream style canned corn
1 egg
¹/₂ teaspoon salt
¹/₄ teaspoon freshly ground white pepper, optional

1. To prepare the *chipotles*, reconstitute in a teaspoon of vinegar with water to cover; then simmer until soft, 5 minutes in the microwave or 30 minutes on top of the range.

2. Butter individual baking dishes (you can use coffee cups if you do not have individual flan dishes). Preheat the oven to 350°.

3. Heat the butter with the milk in a heavy saucepan only until the butter melts. Then place all the ingredients in a blender or food processor and process until well blended. Pour into individual baking dishes.

4. Place the baking dishes in a large baking pan in the preheated oven. Using a pitcher or large measuring cup, pour water into the baking pan to about a 1-inch level. Bake in the oven for 30 minutes, checking for doneness by inserting a sharp knife. If it comes out clean, the custards are done. They should be lightly browned. If not done, continue until they are of the desired brownness. Allow to cool at least 30 minutes before running a sharp knife around each and inverting them onto warm luncheon plates, beside the filet serving.

Spinach Salad with Jícama and Piñon Laced with Raspberry Vinaigrette

Spinach goes so well with beef. Whether it is a souffle, steamed, or creamed, it is an excellent accompaniment. With the corn chipotle flans, this crisp, tartly dressed salad is the perfect complement.

Yield: 4 servings

1 pound fresh spinach leaves, well rinsed
1 cup peeled, diced, jícama
¼ cup piñons
Several grinds black pepper
Raspberry Vinaigrette (see recipe below)

1. Rinse and sort the spinach leaves, discarding the stems and any bad leaves. Spin to dry and place in a salad bowl. Place the jícama in ice water.

2. Toast the piñons a bit in a skillet over medium heat on top of the range until they brown in spots. This should only require a few minutes. Coarsely chop and set aside.

3. Sprinkle several grinds of black pepper or to taste over the spinach. Drizzle with the vinaigrette and toss with the other ingredients. Serve immediately.

Raspberry Vinaigrette

⅓ cup extra, extra virgin olive oil, preferably
  Spanish
⅓ cup raspberry vinegar
⅓ cup blossom honey
1 clove garlic, minced

Place all the ingredients in the order listed in a shaker jar and shake, or place in a shallow bowl, and whisk together. Immediately drizzle over the salad.

Hot, Hot Frosted Fudge Brownies

These are double rich with chocolate and almost fudge-like. The heat of the caribe chile makes them totally unique. They can be frozen for at least 90 days.

Yield: 8 to 12 brownies

2 1-ounce squares unsweetened chocolate
½ cup sweet (unsalted) butter
2 eggs
1 cup granulated sugar
1 tablespoon molasses
1 teaspoon Mexican vanilla
½ cup all-purpose flour
1 tablespoon caribe (crushed northern
    New Mexico chile)
¼ teaspoon salt
½ cup pecans or other nut, chopped
1 recipe frosting (see recipe below)

1. Lightly butter a 9 x 9-inch square baking pan. Preheat the oven to 350°. Melt 2 squares of the chocolate with the butter over low heat, stirring frequently. Using a mixer or food processor, beat the eggs; add the sugar, molasses, and vanilla; mix well on medium speed.

2. Add the butter-chocolate mixture. Add the flour, chile, salt, and nuts and mix well. Pour into the baking pan, smoothing the batter to the edges in an even layer. Bake 20 minutes or until an inserted knife or toothpick comes out clean. Cool on a rack. When cool to the touch, prepare the frosting, or freeze at this point and frost a day before serving.

Cooked Frosting

1½ cups sugar
⅓ cup sweet (unsalted) butter
½ cup light cream or evaporated milk
1 teaspoon Mexican vanilla
3 squares unsweetened chocolate
½ teaspoon caribe (crushed northern
    New Mexico chile)

1. Combine the sugar, butter, and milk in a heavy 3-quart saucepan. Bring to a boil over medium high heat. Have ready a small clear glass bowl with cold water in it.

2. Cook and stir until the mixture holds a soft ball form when tested in the cold water. Cool the saucepan in a sink or pan of cold water; remove pan from water and add the vanilla. Beat until creamy. Frost the brownies. Meanwhile, heat the 3 squares of chocolate until well melted.

3. When the frosting has set a bit, drizzle uniformly with the melted chocolate. Sprinkle the top with the chile. Chill until set. Warm at room temperature, slice, and serve.

Old El Paso Border Dinner

❧

M E N U

Tortilla Avocado Soup

Frijoles Negros Tostaditas

*Chorizo and Piñon Nut-Stuffed
Loin of Pork*

*Tiny Green Beans and Baby Red Potatoes
in Salsa Vinaigrette*

Apricot-Almond Sherry Custard Trifle

Cabernet Sauvignon

Coffee

❧

When the cold chill of winter hangs heavily—clutching onto all life, inspiring us to warm ourselves—what better time to enjoy a subtly spiced menu such as this? This menu is perfect for entertaining business or social friends comfortably, yet with a flair.

While all the recipes in this menu are original, they show a clear Mexican influence. The *tostaditas* are similar to *nachos*, yet much more Latin in both flavor and appearance. The pork roast features a truly spectacular looking and tasting treatment of a meat that can all too often be prepared indifferently. Leftovers freeze and reheat well. The salsa-laden garden vegetable salad complements the roast. The finale takes its inspiration from English trifle as well as the traditional New Mexican/Spanish *natillas* custard. Select a fine bottle of dry red wine, such as Cabernet Sauvignon, to place this dinner in the VSOP class.

For the centerpiece, select a cactus arrangement or dried leaves or even a favorite southwestern sculpture. White or off-white linens—even lace—make a dressy statement on the table.

MENU PLAN

Four hours before:

Stuff the pork loin, truss it, and place it in the oven.

Prepare the Apricot-Almond Sherry Custard Trifle.

After the first hour of roasting, coat the pork with the jalapeño jelly; continue basting every 15 minutes.

Prepare the soup (except for the garnish).

Make the salsa vinaigrette for the salad. Prepare the beans and potatoes and dress with the vinaigrette about an hour before serving.

Prepare the filling ingredients for the tostaditas about 1 hour before guests arrive.

Fry the tortillas.

Set out the coffeemaker.

At serving time:

Assemble the tostaditas and serve them warm.

Cube the avocado for the soup. Then serve.

Slice the pork roast and serve, with the pan juices in a side dish. Serve the bean and potato salad alongside.

Serve the trifle with coffee.

Tortilla Avocado Soup

Tortilla soup, sometimes called Sopa de Ajo *or* Garlic Soup, *has many different versions.*
I prefer the rich broth seething with garlic and chiles and thickened with tortillas.

Yield: 6 to 8 servings

4 cloves garlic, roasted and chopped

1 tablespoon plus 1 teaspoon virgin olive oil,
    preferably Spanish

5 corn tortillas, torn into small pieces

6 cups rich chicken stock, preferably homemade,
    or good quality canned with low salt

2 teaspoons dried chipotle (smoked jalapeño)
    chile, reconstituted and minced

1 ripe avocado

1 fresh lime, juiced

2 teaspoons ground pure mild chile for garnish

6 to 8 whole cilantro leaves, for garnish

1. Use previously roasted garlic or rub the garlic cloves with 1 teaspoon olive oil, wrap in foil and roast while pork is roasting. The garlic is done when soft, about 30 minutes.

2. Place 1 tablespoon oil in heavy saucepan and heat over medium heat. Then add the tortilla pieces and cook and stir until they are somewhat toasted. Add the stock and the roasted, chopped garlic. Add the chipotle chile and cook and stir and simmer together for about 30 minutes.

3. Just before serving, peel the avocado and dice into ½ inch squares. Sprinkle with some of the fresh lime juice. Serve the soup in heated bowls, garnished with avocado cubes, sprinkled with a bit of fresh lime juice and a sprinkle of chile. Float a cilantro leaf on the top of each serving.

Note: For a heartier soup, 2 to 3 cups chicken chunks, as well as root vegetables such as carrots and parsnips, and celery, can be added.

Frijoles Negros Tostaditas

With their black bean topping, these little gems are more Latin American in flavor than southwestern. Black beans—frijoles negros—are increasingly gaining favor as an alternative to the predictable pinto, as their rich, assertive taste is a splendid partner for spicy accompaniments. I always add the Cuban touch of a splash of rum or sherry and squeeze a fresh lime—an idea used most often in black bean soup.

Yield: 8 servings, 32 tostaditas

1 pint corn oil, optional (see **Note**)
8 corn tortillas, preferably blue (standard size— 5⅞" diameter)
2 tablespoons butter, bacon drippings, or lard
2 large garlic cloves, finely minced
1 large Spanish onion, finely chopped
2 cans (1 pound each) black beans, or refried black beans
1 teaspoon salt
1 tablespoon rum or sherry
1 teaspoon fresh lime juice
1 bunch watercress, rinsed and stems removed
5 radishes, sliced thin
¼ cup green onions (scallions), cut crosswise into thin rounds
½ cup sour cream
½ cup coarsely grated Monterey Jack cheese, optional

1. If frying the tortillas, heat the corn oil in a deep skillet to 375°. While the oil is heating, line a cookie sheet with several layers of paper towels for draining. Cut each tortilla into four equal parts, cutting not quite to the center, so that the tortilla can be fried as one piece. Fry each tortilla until crisp, watching for the bubbles to subside before turning to fry the second side. Drain. Tap each tortilla in the center to separate them into 4 pieces. (See *Note* if you prefer to bake them.)

2. In a heavy frying pan, heat the butter. Add the garlic, and as it begins to turn golden, toss in the onion and cook and stir until it becomes clear. Add the beans and mash with a potato masher or large heavy spoon until they are completely pureed. (If using refried black beans, you will not need to mash them). Season with the salt, rum, and lime juice to taste.

3. If the beans seem too dry, add a few drops of hot water. They should be about the texture of heavy pudding so they can be spread on the fried tortillas.

4. To combine, carefully spread a layer of the beans on each tortilla just before serving. Then sprinkle sprigs of watercress over the top of each, add a few disks of radish and a toss of scallion rounds, and center each with 1 tablespoon sour cream topped with 2 tablespoons grated cheese, if using.

Note: You can use commercially fried or baked tostados, or bake quartered tortillas 10 to 15 minutes in a 400° oven until crisp. In either case, the oil can be omitted.

Chorizo and Piñon Nut-Stuffed Loin of Pork

Glorious to behold! The red-hued, chile-laden chorizo *(Mexican sausage) rolled inside the silken pink-white of the pork roast—crusty with a jalapeño jelly glaze—makes for an inimitably elegant entrée.*

Yield: 8 servings

3¹/₂ to 4¹/₂ pounds boneless, butterflied loin of pork
¹/₄ teaspoon salt
1¹/₂ pounds chorizo (see Note)
¹/₂ cup piñons (pine nuts)
1¹/₂ cups (12 ounces) jalapeño jelly, hot or mild,
*   depending on your taste (see page 26)*

1. Lay the pork roast out flat, with the inside (the side from which the bone was removed) facing up. Remove *chorizo* from its casing, then lightly sauté it, breaking it up with a spatula as it cooks. Cook only until about half done, just enough to melt the fat (3¹/₂ minutes or less on medium heat). Drain the sausage meat well, patting it dry with a paper towel, and place it in a bowl. Mix the piñon nuts evenly with the *chorizo* and lay the mixture in a long roll on the inside of the roast. If using Italian sausage (see *Note*), blend in the seasonings before adding the nuts.

2. Bring the two sides together lengthwise. Tie at 1-inch intervals with white cotton twine. Place on a baking sheet.

3. Put the roast in the oven and turn to 350°. After the first hour, spread Homemade Jalapeño Jelly on the outside of the roast. Return the meat to the oven and roast, basting every 15 minutes. Continue roasting for 1¹/₂ to 2 hours more, or until the roast reaches 170° on a meat thermometer. Reserve the juices, skimming the fat, and serve on the side.

Note: If you can't find *chorizo*, substitute hot Italian sausage and add ¹/₂ teaspoon ground cumin and ¹/₂ teaspoon crushed Mexican oregano. If hot Italian sausage is not available, use fresh pork sausage and add 2 to 4 tablespoons of caribe or other crushed dried red chile, plus the cumin and Mexican oregano.

Tiny Green Beans and Baby Red Potatoes
in Salsa Vinaigrette

What was once the bounty of early spring in the Southwest can now be enjoyed all year. Prepared this way, a pair of favorite vegetables have a Tex-Mex tang and can accompany a wide variety of southwestern menus. You can vary the type of salsa here to suit your palate and the other dishes in your meal.

Yield: 8 servings

16 tiny red potatoes, well scrubbed and with a ½-inch belt of skin removed
1½ pounds fresh small green beans, rinsed with stems removed, leaving tips
1 cup water
¼ cup white vinegar
¼ cup extra virgin olive oil, preferably Spanish
½ cup Fresh Garden Salsa (page 31) or to taste
8 fluffy red lettuce leaves, rinsed
16 thin strips of red bell pepper

1. Prepare the vegetables. In a saucepan bring water about one inch deep to a boil. Add the potatoes and green beans and cover. Simmer about 5 minutes, or until the potatoes are just tender, not mushy. Peek once or twice to be sure the water has not evaporated.

2. Combine the vinegar, oil, and salsa. When the vegetables are just done (do not overcook!) drain excess liquid and cover and allow to dry out on the surface over a low flame—about 5 minutes.

3. Toss with the vinaigrette; keep tossing every 15 minutes or so until the vegetables have absorbed most of the liquid. After about an hour, place the lettuce leaves on individual plates, then arrange the green beans and potatoes in an attractive pattern. Garnish with a criss-cross of bell pepper strips and chill.

Apricot-Almond Sherry Custard Trifle

Along the border, soft custards combined with fruits are a very popular dessert, as they are soothing to the system after a series of intensely spicy dishes. You can vary this basic recipe with different combinations of fruits—currant jam and fresh strawberries are a delicious pair. For calorie counting, omit the cake, double the custard portion, and serve layered with apricot jam, almonds, and stewed apricots.

Yield: 8 servings

1¾ cups milk
⅓ cup sugar
Pinch of salt
¼ cup flour
2 eggs, separated
1 egg white
2 teaspoons plus ½ cup cream sherry
Several gratings of fresh nutmeg
    (⅛ teaspoon ground)
1 sponge cake layer, 10 inches in diameter
½ cup apricot jam
2 tablespoons toasted slivered almonds
12 large, extra fancy dried apricots stewed
    in ½ cup water

1. Place the milk in a heavy 2-quart saucepan. Stir in the sugar and salt. Place over low heat and cook and stir until the sugar dissolves. Spoon out about ½ cup of the warm milk mixture into a small bowl and let it cool.

2. Carefully sprinkle the flour over the cooled mixture. Stir, and when well blended, add the egg yolks and stir well. Add to the remaining cooled milk mixture.

3. Cook over low heat, stirring constantly, until very well blended. Continue to cook until the mixture thickens and coats the back of a spoon. Cool slightly. Stir periodically.

4. Meanwhile, beat the 3 egg whites until very stiff, adding the 2 teaspoons sherry and the nutmeg while beating. Fold into the cooled yolk-milk mixture.

5. While waiting for the yolk mixture to cool, place the sponge cake on a large serving platter. Sprinkle with the remaining ½ cup sherry and allow to marinate until the custard is done. Then spread with the apricot jam.

6. Place a uniform layer of the slivered almonds on top. Pour the custard over the cake. Garnish with the stewed, cooled apricots, placing 4 in the center and the remaining 8 evenly around the edge.

7. To serve, slice into 8 wedges, being certain to center an apricot on each and to get half of one at the narrow end of each slice.

Après Ski

M E N U

Hot Buttered Rum

Janet's Chile Meatballs with Caliente Dip

Enchiladas Suizas

Chablis

Manzanos en Crisp

Following any kind of winter activity, nothing could be more satisfying than spicy, filling south western food. Here is a menu designed for entertaining hungry, cold, weary guests, giving them instant gratification and sparing the cook any frantic last-minute preparation. All the dishes in the meal can be prepared well in advance and easily heated just before serving. While you and your guests are warming up, the foods will be too, soon ready for serving in front of a fire or around a big kitchen or dining room table.

The chile meatballs are a delicious appetizer, perfect with hot buttered rum, and especially memorable grilled in a fireplace over a hibachi. The Enchiladas Suizas recipe has been adapted to use easily available ingredients and suffers not a bit from advance preparation—even freezing. The Manzanos en Crisp also bears up wonderfully well under the same treatment. Served warm with whipped cream or rich vanilla ice cream, it is, to quote my father, "food for the gods."

Keep the decor rustic and minimal. I always like to serve a meal like this on a quilt, either on the floor in front of the fire or simply on the table. Use calico or gingham napkins and tin or pottery plates. Lacking any fresh flowers, create a centerpiece of waxy vegetables or fresh fruits.

One day before (or up to three months in advance):

Prepare the batter for the Hot Buttered Rum
and refrigerate.

Prepare and bake the meatballs. Refrigerate
or freeze.

Prepare the Enchiladas Suizas and refrigerate
or freeze.

Two hours before:

Chill the wine.

Make the dip for the meatballs.

Prepare the Manzanos en Crisp.

Place the meatballs out for grilling or broiling.

Preheat the oven for the Enchiladas Suizas and
Manzanos en Crisp.

At serving time:

Broil the meatballs and serve with the dip and
Hot Buttered Rum.

Meanwhile, bake the Enchiladas Suizas and
Manzanos en Crisp.

Serve the enchiladas piping hot with the wine,
then serve the dessert.

Hot Buttered Rum

After skiing, sledding, ice skating or almost any cold, snowy, robust activity is the perfect time for really good "hot buttereds." Although this recipe is for one drink, because it should ideally be prepared individually, you can make several at a time by stirring up a batch of the batter (multiply the ingredient measurements accordingly) and keeping it handy in the refrigerator.

Yield: One 8-ounce drink

*1 tablespoon sweet (unslated) butter,
    at room temperature*
1/2 tablespoon dark brown sugar
1/8 teaspoon ground cinnamon
Few gratings of fresh nutmeg
1/2 teaspoon Grand Marnier
2 whole cloves
2 ounces dark rum
1 cup boiling water
1 Cinnamon stick
Orange peel, cut in one long strip, optional

1. For batter: In a small bowl, combine the butter, brown sugar, cinnamon, nutmeg, and Grand Marnier until well blended. (If you wish to prepare a quantity of the batter, increase the amounts of each of the ingredients proportionally, and refrigerate until used.)

2. Place about 1½ tablespoons of the batter in each mug and add the whole cloves, rum, and boiling water. Stir until well blended. Garnish with a cinnamon stick and strip of orange peel.

Janet's Chile Meatballs

Janet Beers Pugh, my childhood friend whom I lured to New Mexico in 1966 and who is now a confirmed New Mexican, developed these for a party. I liked them so much that she generously shared the recipe. They are a snappy variation on Swedish meatballs and as they can be frozen for at least 3 months, are an especially convenient appetizer. Vary the dipping sauce, if you wish—use your favorite salsa, chile con queso, or even guacamole.

Yield: 6 generous servings

2 egg yolks or 1 whole egg
1/2 cup dry bread crumbs
1 cup sharp cheddar cheese, grated
2 tablespoons pure ground red chile (use the type you prefer—I like southern New Mexico hot)
1 teaspoon salt
1 pound lean ground beef

1. Preheat the oven to 350°. If using the yolks, beat together with 1/2 cup water. If using a whole egg, use 1/3 cup water.

2. Add the rest of the ingredients and lightly mix together. Form 1-inch meatballs and place on a jelly roll tin or large 9x13 inch loaf pan. Bake 10 minutes, then drain well on paper towels and let cool.

3. These can be prepared ahead and left to await the serving hour, or they can be frozen in rigid containers in layers with wax paper between.

4. To serve, broil over a hibachi in the fireplace on long skewers, or under the broiler in your oven.

5. Serve hot and crisp with the following sauce or one of your selection.

Caliente Dip

2 hot red pickled cherry peppers (see Note)
2 whole pickled hot jalapeño chiles
1/2 cup halved and thinly sliced stuffed green olives
1/2 cup thinly sliced pitted black olives
1/2 cup extra virgin olive oil, preferably Spanish

Combine all the ingredients and bring to a simmer. Serve hot as a dip for the meatballs. Even better, serve an additional dip or two—perhaps one mild creamy one and another spicy but cold one.

Note: You can substitute pickled jalapeños, using 2 teaspoons minced.

Enchiladas Suizas

I developed this adaptation of one of the most popular southwestern dishes with south-of-the-border origins to use green chiles, which are more easily available than the traditionally used tomatillos. Although canned chiles are acceptable, fresh ones or those you have parched and frozen have much better flavor. Always cook the chicken yourself so that you have the wonderfully rich stock to use for creating the sauce. (See next page for step-by-step instructions.)

Yield: 6 servings

THE CHICKEN

3 chicken thighs and legs, or 2 chicken breasts
1 large carrot, cut into thirds*
1 celery rib, quartered*
1 medium Spanish onion, coarsely chopped
1 teaspoon dried thyme, crumbled*
1/2 teaspoon salt*

   *Variation: For extra flavorful chicken use chicken stock instead of the water and asterisked ingredients.

THE CASSEROLE

12 corn tortillas
The cooked chicken, removed from the bones and "pulled" or shredded
2 cups coarsely grated Monterey Jack and sharp full cream cheddar, tossed together
1 cup whipping cream
1/4 cup finely chopped purple Spanish onion

THE SAUCE

2 tablespoons sweet butter
4 tablespoons flour
2 cups rich chicken stock from cooking the chicken
1 tablespoon coarsely chopped fresh cilantro
1/2 cup chopped green chiles (3 to 4 parched and peeled, page 17)

THE GARNISH

2 teaspoons caribe (crushed northern New Mexican chile)
Several whole springs fresh cilantro

1. Place all the chicken ingredients in a large pot, add water (or stock) barely to cover the tips of the meat, cover, and simmer until the chicken is tender. When the chicken is done, the bones should wiggle and the meat should be very tender to the touch of a fork (about 35 to 45 minutes).

2. Meanwhile, prepare the sauce. Melt the butter, add the flour, and stir together until slightly brown. Then slowly stir in the chicken stock, a little at a time, until a rich, thick sauce develops. Stir in the cilantro and the green chiles. Taste and adjust the seasonings.

3. When the chicken is cool enough to touch, remove the skin and bones and shred the meat. Set aside. Strain the stock and skim off the fat.

4. Dip each tortilla into the sauce, place a strip of the cooked chicken and a sprinkle of the cheeses in the center, and roll, placing them seam side down in a casserole, preferably an authentic Mexican one.

5. When all are rolled, distribute the remaining sauce and cheese evenly over the tortillas. Pour the cream evenly over the entire casserole. Top with a ribbon of the coarsely chopped onion.

6. Either freeze for up to 3 months, well covered in moisture-proof packaging, or bake immediately in a 350° oven for 20 minutes. Serve piping hot.

Note: If frozen, bake 30 to 40 minutes or until bubbling hot. If you have trouble rolling the tortillas, you can fry them in oil, drain and then proceed.

Manzanas en Crisp

A year-round favorite with our family, this apple crisp recipe takes advantage of winter apples. Bake the crisp ahead and warm it in the oven after removing the enchiladas, or bake it along with them. It's a good traveler and keeper, and any leftovers will freeze quite well. The crisp will not suffer if it is frozen whole after baking, either. Serve with whipped cream or vanilla ice cream, if desired.

Yield: 6 servings

1½ cups light brown sugar
1½ cups flour
½ teaspoon ground cinnamon
¼ teaspoon freshly grated nutmeg
¾ cup unsalted sweet butter
¼ cup toasted piñon nuts
5 medium or 4 large cooking apples such as
*   Golden Delicious, Jonathan, or Macintosh,*
*   peeled and cut into thick slices (about 4 cups)*
2 teaspoons lemon juice

1. Mix the dry ingredients together and cut in the butter with a pastry blender. Combine in a food processor or mixer until it is like coarse meal. Toast the piñon nuts in a heavy skillet on top of the range until golden.

2. Spread the apple slices on the bottom of a buttered 9 x 9-inch baking dish. Sprinkle with the lemon juice, then the crumb mixture. Bake at 350° until the fruit is soft and the crumbs are browned, 35 to 40 minutes. If desired, serve with sweetened whipped cream or French vanilla ice cream.

Late Night's Pleasure

M E N U

Champagne

Avocado Torta Salada

Chimis Maximos

*Mint Chocolate Mousse
with Chocolate Fudge Sauce*

This menu for late-night dining after an evening out was developed for those who agree that living well is the best revenge. There is nothing tired or predictable here: showy, spicy first courses are followed by a refreshing fillip of dark chocolate mousse tinged with mint. You'll never be lonely!

Popping the cork on the champagne just as soon as your guests arrive will keep them pleasantly occupied while you quickly make the guacamole and assemble the torta, which doubles as an appetizer and salad. Then fry or bake the *chimis* and presto—you can be your own party guest.

Serve this dinner informally in a cozy, comfortable area, such as before a fireplace, which provides the ideal winter background. Simple table settings are best here. All you need are large napkins wrapped around the silverware.

MENU PLAN

Day before (or several days before):

Prepare the Carne Adobado for the Chimis Maximos.

Fry the tostados for the torta.

Make the Chocolate Fudge Sauce.

Early in the day:

Chill the champagne.

Fill and roll the chimis.

Make the mousse, spoon into individual parfait or sherbet glasses, and chill.

Whip the cream and chill.

Prepare the ingredients for the torta.

At serving time:

Serve the champagne while you heat the tostados, make the guacamole, and assemble the torta.

Fry or bake the chimis and serve with the torta.

Warm the Chocolate Fudge Sauce. Top the individual mousses with whipped cream and créme de menthe. Serve with the sauce.

Avocado Torta Salada

This novel and attractive way to serve guacamole, the all-time favorite Tex-Mex salad or dip, involves forming a torta by layering the guacamole with warm tostados and crisp, crunchy vegetables. Though it must be assembled at the very last moment, it can be prepared in minutes if you ready all the ingredients ahead.

Yield: 6 servings

1 quart cooking oil
12 corn tortillas
3 ripe avocados, preferably the Haas variety
*   with the black nubby skins*
1 cup finely chopped red Spanish onions
1 medium red ripe tomato, peeled and chopped
*   medium fine*
2 garlic cloves, finely minced
1 fresh jalapeño chile, very finely minced
Juice of 1 lime
1 teaspoon salt
2 tablespoons cilantro, coarsely chopped, optional
12 cherry tomatoes, halved
1 each green, yellow, red bell pepper,
*   cut in ½-inch-wide strips*

1. Heat the cooking oil to 375° in an electric fryer or cooking pot.

2. Fry 2 whole tortillas and quarter the remaining 10, using a sharp knife or scissors to make 4 deep cuts almost to the center, dividing each into fourths. Do not cut apart as they will be much easier to fry. When crisply fried, remove and drain. When slightly cooled, tap the center portion and they will quickly fall into fourths (tostados). Lightly salt.

3. Just before serving, warm the tostados for 15 minutes in a 350° oven while making the guacamole. Cut each avocado in half and scoop the flesh into a bowl. Coarsely chop the avocado using two knives, then add ½ cup of the onion, ¼ cup chopped tomato, garlic, and jalapeño to taste. Add lime juice to taste and ¾ teaspoon salt. Lightly fold together, taking care not to crush or mash the avocado. Fold in the cilantro, if using.

4. Arrange the torta by placing one of the flat, crisply fried tortillas on an attractive serving plate. Top with about one third of the guacamole, then add a sprinkle of the remaining chopped red onion and a few of the cherry tomato halves. Add the other fried tortilla, making a sandwich, and top with the remaining guacamole. Garnish with the rest of the chopped onion, some of the other tomato halves, tostados and the strips of pepper to make an artistic arrangement. The remaining tomato, peppers, and tostados should be scattered around the plate to create an attractive presentation. To serve, either allow guests to eat the top layer and break the whole crisp-fried tortilla tostados into pieces or cut into sixths and arrange on 6 individual plates.

Chimis Maximos

Maximo in the name of this recipe for wonderful-tasting, crisp chimis refers not only to their being about as good as you'll ever eat, but also to the fact that they are truly maximally filled—with carne adobado, a personal favorite. If you can't find 12-inch tortillas, adjust the amount of each filling accordingly. (Chimi, short for chimichango, is actually a fried burrito.)

Yield: 6 servings (double for hearty appetites)

6 cups Carne Adobado (recipe follows)
1½ cups cooked pinto beans
1½ teaspoons butter or lard
1 large garlic clove, finely minced
1 cup finely chopped Spanish onion, divided
6 wheat tortillas—12 inches in diameter,
    or largest available
1 cup coarsely grated cheddar and Monterey
    Jack cheeses, mixed
1 quart cooking oil, optional
8 ounces sour cream
6 lettuce leaves, coarsely torn (use red leaf or a
    bright green leafy lettuce, not iceberg)
6 cherry tomatoes, halved or made into tomato roses
1 cup Cold Salsa Verde (see page 32)
1 cup Santa Fe Salsa (see page 33)

1. Prepare the Carne Adobado the night before, or up to three months ahead and freeze. Refry the pinto beans by placing the 1½ teaspoons butter or lard in a heavy skillet; when melted, add the garlic. When it begins to turn golden, add 1 tablespoon of the finely chopped onion and cook until it begins to soften; then add the beans and mash and fry until the mixture becomes stiff and almost dry.

2. Warm the wheat tortillas to room temperature. If not extremely fresh, steam slightly in a steamer or put in the microwave oven for 15 seconds each. Preheat the oil to 375°, or, if baking rather than frying the chimis, heat the oven to 400°.

3. Place ¼ cup warm refried beans on each tortilla, working with one at a time. Add 1 cup carne adobado and 2 to 3 tablespoons chopped onion and 3 tablespoons grated cheeses. Roll each as for a blintz, bringing the bottom over the filling with about one fourth of a tortilla overlap. Then fold the tortilla in from each side. Fold the top down over the filling and secure with toothpicks. Set aside. These can be filled and rolled up to 12 hours in advance.

4. Bake for 12 to 15 minutes or until the chimis are crisp and golden. Or deep-fry in 375° oil or lard until each is golden brown. Drain on absorbent towels.

5. Garnish with ribbons of sour cream. Garnish the plates with lettuce and tomato halves.

Carne Adobado

This is one of the best, if not the very best-tasting pork creations from northern New Mexico. Traceable to Conquistador days, this dish has somehow never gained the favor it deserves. I always make a full six-pound recipe, because I like to have lots available for burritos, tacos, enchiladas, main dish servings, or to heap over rice, beans, or eggs.

Yield: 3 ½ quarts

½ cup caribe (crushed dried red chile)
¼ cup ground pure California or mild red chile
¼ cup ground pure southern New Mexico hot chile
3 large garlic cloves, crushed
2 tablespoons freshly ground cumin
2 tablespoons freshly ground Mexican oregano
2 teaspoons salt
4 cups water
6 pounds bone-in shoulder or loin pork chops, cut ½ inch thick (trimmed so as to keep a narrow layer of fat around the edges)

1. Combine all the ingredients except the pork chops in an electric blender to create a thick sauce. Then pour a layer of sauce into a large flat glass baking dish. Layer the pork chops on top of the marinade and repeat, adding sauce and chops until all the chops are coated on both sides. Let marinate 2 hours at room temperature, periodically spooning the chile mixture over the top and turning the chops over. Refrigerate overnight. (The pork can be frozen for up to 3 months at this point.)

2. In the morning, stir and coat each pork chop with chile sauce. Bake at 325°, covered with a lid or foil for the first 45 minutes. Remove the cover and bake another hour or hour and a half, spooning the sauce over the chops every 30 minutes.

3. Let cool on the counter. Using a sharp knife, remove the bones and pull the meat apart with your fingers to shred the pork. Place the shredded meat back in the sauce in the baking dish. Return to the oven to allow the sauce to cook in—about 30 minutes or until it is thick but not dry. When done, the pork should be a bright rosy red color and the meat should be very tender.

Mint Chocolate Mousse

This is enormously soothing as a finishing touch after foods that are seethingly hot—which the chimis certainly can be. Make the mousse up to 6 hours ahead, then serve in parfait glasses with a dollop of whipped cream swished with a drizzle of créme de menthe, and with the Chocolate Fudge Sauce that follows.

Yield: 6 servings

6 squares good quality semisweet chocolate
³/₈ cup water
6 eggs, separated
³/₄ cup plus 2 tablespoons superfine sugar
¹/₄ cup heavy cream
2 tablespoons white crème de menthe, plus
*   additional for pouring over the top; if preferred,*
*   use green for the topping*
Chocolate Fudge Sauce (recipe follows)

1. Combine the chocolate and water in the top of a double boiler or place over low heat and melt, stirring occasionally, yet watching carefully to prevent burning. When melted, set aside.

2. Beat the egg whites in a large bowl until very stiff, making sure that there is no fat of any kind on the beaters or in the whites, as it will prevent stiff whites.

3. Place the yolks in a large bowl, then add ³/₄ cup sugar very gradually, continuing to beat until thick and lemon colored. Add the cooled, melted chocolate and beat until well blended.

4. Stir about 1 cup of the egg whites into the chocolate mixture, then blend well. Add this mixture to the rest of the egg whites, using a rubber scraper to fold the two mixtures together to form a very smooth chocolatey mixture.

5. Serve with dollops of whipped cream (made by beating the heavy cream with 2 tablespoons superfine sugar) drizzled with a few drops of crème de menthe on the side, as well as the warm Chocolate Fudge Sauce, for guests to help themselves.

Chocolate Fudge Sauce

This creamy, rich sauce is best served slightly warm over the mousse. If there's any left, reheat it carefully and you have a fondue for fresh fruits: strawberries, bananas, and squares of pineapple.

Yield: 6 to 8 servings

6 squares good quality unsweetened chocolate
1 cup half and half
1¹/₂ cups sugar
¹/₄ pound sweet (unsalted) butter
¹/₈ teaspoon salt
2 teaspoons vanilla
¹/₂ teaspoon ground cinnamon
1¹/₂ ounces Kahlua

1. Place all the ingredients in a small heavy saucepan and heat over medium-low heat, stirring frequently.

2. Cook and stir until the chocolate melts; then reduce the heat to low and continue cooking for 5 minutes more. Allow to set at room temperature; then warm over low heat to serve with the mousse.

Index